The Second
How-To Handbook
for
Jewish Living

The Second
How-To Handbook
for
Jewish Living

**Rabbi Kerry M. Olitzky
and
Rabbi Ronald H. Isaacs**

Illustrated by
Dorcas Gelabert

KTAV Publishing House, Inc.
Hoboken, New Jersey

Library of Congress Cataloging-in-Publication Data

Olitzky, Kerry M.
    The second how-to handbook for Jewish living / Kerry M. Olitzky and
Ronald H. Isaacs.
        p.   cm.
    ISBN 0–88125–534–3. — ISBN 0–88125–550–5 (pbk.)
    1. Judaism—customs and practices. 2. Jewish way of life.
I. Isaacs, Ronald H. II. Title.
BM700.O435   1996
296.7'.4—dc20   95-46769
                                                                          CIP

Manufactured in the United States of America
KTAV Publishing House, 900 Jefferson Street, Hoboken NJ, 07030

Introduction

Why a second book of How To's, yet another book about basic Jewish practice? That's what people want to know. The answer is simple. Judaism is more than just knowing. It is about doing. No matter how much you think you know, there is always more to experience in Judaism. It's one of the many reasons that study is so important. Jewish study teaches you about "real knowledge," the stuff you really want to know in life. Through Jewish practice, you will come to know more.

However, practice will generally lead you to more questions, as well. That's precisely how this second volume of *The "How To" Handbook for Jewish Living* came to be. After the wide circulation of the first volume, in a variety of settings, people asked us for more guidance about Jewish practice. Thus, in some areas, this volume presents more basic Judaism in a readily accessible format. However, in most cases, this book presents the reader with a second level of Jewish practice. In other words, once you feel comfortable with basic Jewish practice, here's more for you to try. Our goal is simple. We believe that Jewish practice brings you closer to God—and closer to yourself.

Rabbi Kerry M. Olitzky
Rabbi Ronald H. Isaacs

Table of Contents

Giving a *Devar Torah*
דְּבַר תּוֹרָה

The source:

Understood in general terms as a short sermon, the precise origin of the *devar Torah* (literally "a word of Torah") is not clear. It is probably a very old form of exposition which dates back to the *targum,* the translation of the Torah into the vernacular Aramaic. Remember: all translation is interpretation.

What you need to know:

1. Since a *devar Torah* reflects your understanding of a particular text or selection from the Bible, begin there. Review the text in context in order to understand what it meant for the biblical writer.

2. Review the classical commentary of Rashi, available in various editions in English, as a means of accessing the tradition's clear understanding of the portion of text. Rashi is encyclopedic (and pre–CD ROM!) in his approach to the history of Jewish tradition.

3. Now enter the text on your own. Grapple with the struggle of the character in the Bible. Ask yourself, "How do his or her issues of faith impact on my own?" This is where Torah offers ultimate meaning to you as an individual.

4. Now you can write down your thoughts. Don't try to tell the listeners everything you know about Torah and Judaism. There will be plenty of other times for that. Just tell them what you want them to know. Be brief. Like any good composition, make sure there is a logical flow from the introduction through the conclusion. Remember that oral presentations require a different style than written presentations.

5. If you are comfortable in doing so, use the *devar Torah* as a way of engaging the community in dialogue.

6. When speaking to young children, try to be concrete. Avoid abstractions. Feel free to use props, puppets, and visual aids.

Things to remember:

1. While the modern synagogue has championed freedom of the pulpit, do not use the pulpit as a vehicle to force your political views on others.

2. Speak slowly, clearly, and emphatically. Make good eye contact with your listeners.

3. Study. The more you learn, the more you will have to say.

4. Listen. The more you hear others offer *divrei Torah,* the more comfortable you will be delivering your own. Remember: don't compare yourself to others. Develop your own unique style.

5. Remember whatever you have to say: Jewish tradition teaches us that words from the heart enter the heart.

Key words and phrases:

Darshan דַּרְשָׁן. Preacher.
Drash דְּרָשׁ. Central idea in the explanation of the sacred text under discussion.
Drasha דְּרָשָׁה. Sermon. May be used almost interchange-ably with *devar Torah.*
Maggid מַגִּיד. Person who tells stories/parables in order to teach lessons from the biblical text.
Musar מוּסָר. Ethical lesson derived from the text.
Vort (Yiddish) וואָרט. Literally, "a word"; reflects the same sense as *devar Torah.*

If you want to know more:

The American Rabbi (periodical).
Bradley Shavit Artson, "Delivering the Classical D'var Torah." In *Proceedings of the 1993 Convention, The Rabbinical Assembly* (New York, 1993).
Israel Bettan, *Studies in Jewish Preaching* (Cincinnati, 1939).
Solomon Freehof, *Modern Jewish Preaching* (Cincinnati, 1941).

Richard Israel, *The Kosher Pig* (Los Angeles, 1993). (See chapter "How to Give a Devar Torah.")

Bruce Kadden and Barbara Kadden, *Teaching Tefillah: Insights and Activities on Prayer* (Denver, 1994).

Joel Rosenberg, "Giving a Devar Torah." In *The Second Jewish Catalog,* edited by Sharon Strassfeld and Michael Strassfeld (Philadelphia, 1976).

Arranging *Aliyot*
or, How to Be a *Gabbai*
עֲלִיּוֹת

The source:

Traditionally the *gabbai* was a lay communal official charged with a variety of duties, including the collection of *tzedakah*. In many instances the *gabbai* performed administrative duties in the synagogue comparable to those of the ritual director in the modern Jewish house of worship. Nowadays the *gabbai* is most active during the Torah-reading service, making sure that everything runs smoothly, attending to such matters as covering and uncovering the Torah scroll at the appropriate moment, and most especially arranging the *aliyot* and calling individuals to the Torah when it is their turn.

What you need to know:

1. The *gabbai* uncovers the Torah scroll by removing its mantle, breastplate, and crown (or *rimmonim*) when it is brought to the *bimah* after being carried through the congregation in procession.

2. The *gabbai* invites individual worshippers to the Torah honor in accordance with the synagogue's customary practice. In traditional synagogues, a *kohen* (priestly descendant) is invited first, followed by a Levite (assistant priest), and then come the ordinary Israelites. In liberal synagogues, where all worshippers are considered equal, Torah honors are distributed without regard to ancestry.

3. On Shabbat there should be at least seven *aliyot* for the reading, the *maftir*, as well as the honor of lifting the Torah scroll (*hagbahah*) and dressing the Torah scroll (*gelilah*). Make sure that you get the Hebrew names of the individuals to be honored, so that you can call them to the Torah by their Hebrew given names followed by the patronymic "son or daughter of mother/father." If

a Levite is not available, a *kohen* may be called for the second *aliyah*, but a *kohen* may not be called for any of the Israelite *aliyot*.

4. The Torah reader shows the individual called for an *aliyah* the place where the next reading begins. Make sure that the reader moves over slightly so that the *aliyah* honoree can grasp the handles of the Torah scroll and stand in front of it while reciting the blessing.

5. Generally, the *gabbai* covers the Torah scroll with its mantle after the blessing is recited following the reading of the Torah while the next person is called for an *aliyah*. The scroll is also covered during any discussion and during the recitation of a *Misheberach* or any other particular blessing.

6. While at the Torah, hold the *etz chayim* so that the Torah scroll does not move around.

7. Help the reader to roll the Torah scroll at the end of the reading of each column.

8. Follow the reading in the *tikkun* to watch out for mistakes.

9. Assist the persons doing *hagbahah* and *gelilah*.

Things to remember:

1. While some believe that every error in reading the Torah should be corrected, the Torah reading should only be corrected when the reading mistake changes the meaning of the text. In that case the word should be repeated.

2. Whether you use the annual or the triennial cycle for reading, most *Chumashim* will indicate each *aliyah*. At least three verses should be read for each *aliyah*, but the entire reading should not end on an unfavorable topic. This is especially important when you add more honors than the required *aliyot*.

3. While most synagogues have regular routes for reaching the reading table, one is supposed to take the shortest route possible, depending on where the individual is

seated in the synagogue. If the person is equidistant, ascend to the reader's right and descend from the reader's left. Often, out of respect, honorees descend from the pulpit, or leave the reading table, backwards—not wanting to turn their backs on the Torah or the ark.

4. The congregation should stand when the following sections are read: Song of Moses (Exodus 15:1–21); Ten Commandments (Exodus 20:1–14 and Deuteronomy 5:6–18). It is also considered an honor to read these portions before the congregation.

5. The following portions should be read softly, since they reflect the backsliding of our people and God's rebuke: Exodus 32:1–33:6; Leviticus 26:14–43; Numbers 11; and Deuteronomy 28:15–68.

6. While different communities have their own traditions for the musical cantillation of the Torah and Haftarah (which of course are different from each other in all communities), there are also special cantillations for the *megillot* of Esther, Lamentations, Ruth, Ecclesiastes, and Song of Songs. A person who does not read the proper system of cantillations is said to violate the verse, "You shall not move your neighbor's landmarks set up by previous generations" (Deuteronomy 19:14).

7. Traditionally, the third and sixth *aliyot* are reserved for those of great learning and piety, as is the *aliyah* that concludes each of the five books of the Torah.

8. According to Jewish tradition, all those called to the Torah are legal witnesses to the Sinai experience, which we are reenacting by reading the Torah publicly, and therefore the laws concerning witnesses are in force. Thus a father and son may not be called consecutively, nor may two brothers (and we would add sisters). Perhaps this custom is a leftover from the superstition of the evil eye. (*Note:* This tradition is often relaxed in many Reform, Conservative, and Reconstructionist synagogues.)

9. If there are many honors to be given, here is the list of priorities according to Jewish tradition:

    a. Bridegroom (and bride)

b. Bar (and Bat) Mitzvah
c. Baby naming
d. A person commemorating a *Yahrtzeit*
e. A person rising from *shivah*

10. Some congregations have reintroduced the triennial reading of the Torah, whereby only a third of each weekly Torah portion is actually read each year. In this case the *maftir* remains the same each year regardless of what is being read.

11. When in doubt, check with the rabbi or cantor. Some communities, particularly Sephardic ones, have different traditions. For example, there are synagogues where family members rise in deference to the father (or mother) if that individual is given a Torah honor.

12. When calling a rabbi to the honor of the Torah, use the phrase *morenu harav* or *moratenu harav,* "our teacher and rabbi," before the individual's name.

13. When there are more than seven *aliyot* plus the *maftir,* traditionally one pauses before continuing with the next *aliyah.*

Key words and phrases:

Aliyah (plural, *aliyot*) עֲלִיָּה. Literally "going up"; a Torah honor.

Baal koreh בַּעַל-קוֹרֵא. Torah reader.

Hosafot הוֹסָפוֹת. Additional *aliyot* beyond the Shabbat seven plus one (*maftir*).

Maftir מַפְטִיר. Concluding reading, repeating the last few verses of the Torah portion; *aliyah* given to the person who is to read the Haftarah so that he or she does not feel less honored than the Torah reader.

Minyan מִנְיָן. Prayer quorum. Traditionally, ten adult males are required for a *minyan.* In many Conservative congregations, women are included in the *minyan* requirement. Reconstructionist and Reform congregations are egalitarian; the Reform movement does not require a *minyan* for the recitation of any prayer.

Mi she-yirtzah מִי שֶׁיִּרְצֶה. Volunteer, especially one willing to act as *baal koreh* and read the verses of backsliding and rebuke.

Segan סְגָן. The person who stands next to the Torah reader to ensure that no mistakes are made and in addition acts as assistant *gabbai*, handling things at the reading desk. In most synagogues today, no distinction is made between the *gabbai* and the *segan*.

Shliach tzeebur שְׁלִיחַ צִבּוּר. Literally, "messenger of the congregation"; the one who leads the congregation in worship, often the cantor or rabbi.

If you want to know more:

Hayim Halevy Donin, *To Pray as a Jew* (New York, 1980).

"The Geography of the Synagogue," in *The Second Jewish Catalog*, edited by Sharon Strassfeld and Michael Strassfeld (Philadelphia, 1976).

Bruce Kadden and Barbara Kadden. *Teaching Tefillah: Insights and Activities on Prayer* (Denver, 1994).

Earl Klein, *Jewish Prayer: Concepts and Customs* (Columbus, OH, 1986).

Alfred Kolatch, *The Jewish Home Advisor* (New York, 1990).

More particulars:

1. We are taught in the Talmud to rise before those of great learning (Babylonian Talmud, Kiddushin 33b). Since the Torah represents the pinnacle of learning, we rise in its presence. Thus we rise as the Torah scroll is taken from the ark and carried around the sanctuary prior to and following its reading.

2. There are three *aliyot* on normal Torah-reading days (Monday and Thursday) and at the *minchah* (afternoon) service on Shabbat. On new moons and the intermediate days of Passover and Sukkot, there are four *aliyot*. On holidays there are five *aliyot*. On Yom Kippur there are six.

3. The reason the Torah is read at the weekday services on Monday and Thursday as well as on Shabbat is to ensure that we do not go three days in a row without reading the Torah.

How to Tell If a Torah Is Kosher, *Tallit* and *Tefillin* Too!

תּוֹרָה, טַלִּית וּתְפִלִּין

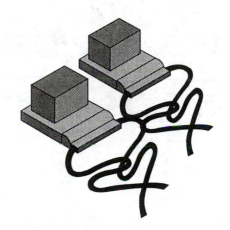

The source:

"Everyone should write his [or her] own Torah scroll" (Babylonian Talmud, Sanhedrin 21b). Since that is not really possible, we invite a scribe (*sofer*) to prepare a scroll on our behalf, sometimes even filling in the letters prepared for us to simulate the writing of a Torah. The word *sofer* comes from the Hebrew root meaning "to count." *Soferim* (plural) learned their trade in families, much like the guilds in ancient Israelite society.

What you need to know:

This is only a guide to help you. For real guidance, consult a trained and skilled *sofer* in your community. If in doubt, contact your local rabbi for help in finding a *sofer*.

1. A Torah scroll is *pasul* (unfit for use) when it contains errors, has faded letters, or the stitching of the pieces of parchment has come undone. In most cases, these things can be repaired by a competent scribe. If the scroll (or *tefillin* or *mezuzah*) cannot be fixed, it must be placed in a *genizah* to be eventually buried properly.

2. The parchment in a *mezuzah* should be examined regularly—twice every seven years.

3. While *tefillin* straps (*retzua, retzuot*) can be easily replaced, the stitching must be removed from the *tefillin* boxes (*batim*), the *bayit shel rosh* (for the head) and the *bayit shel yad* (for the arm), in order for it to be checked properly.

Things to remember:

1. Scribes work on Torah scrolls, *tefillin, mezuzot,* and bills of divorce (*gittin*). Other documents may be handled by a

calligrapher. Therefore, do not make corrections in these things; allow a scribe to do so.

2. Scribes use a feather quill and indelible ink, working in straight lines on specially prepared parchment. Everything they use of animal origin must be kosher.

3. A scribe must properly prepare for the job of writing sacred objects. Traditionally, the scribe goes to a *mikvah* (ritual bath) before starting such holy work.

Key words and phrases:

Get (plural, *gittin*) גֵט. Bill of divorce.

Sofer סוֹפֵר. Scribe.

Sofer stam סוֹפֵר סְתַּ"ם. Acronym from the words *Sefer Torah*, *tefillin*, *mezuzot*. Refers to a traditional Scribe.

Tikkun soferim תִּקוּן סוֹפְרִים. A *sofer*'s copybook, a professional compendium or guide that contains the traditional Torah text (for purposes of writing and correcting Torah scrolls), as well as rules for spacing and flourishes (*tagin*) like crowns. There are also rules which instruct the scribe how to start a column which begins with the Hebrew letter *vav*.

If you want to know more:

J. Simcha Cohen, *The 613th Commandment: An Analysis of the Mitzvah to Write a Sefer Torah* (New York, 1983).

Paul Cowan, *A Torah Is Written* (Philadelphia, 1986).

Alfred Kolatch, *The Jewish Home Advisor* (New York, 1990).

Moses Maimonides, *Hilchot Tefillin Umezuzah V'sefer Torah: The Laws Governing Tefillin, Mezuzah, and Torah* and *Hilchot Tzitzit: The Laws of Tzitzit*. Translated by Eliyahu Touger (Brooklyn, 1990).

Eric Ray, *Sofer: The Story of a Torah Scroll* (Los Angeles, 1986).

Finding Dates on a Hebrew (Soli-Lunar) Calendar
לוּחַ עִבְרִי

The source:

"This month shall be the beginning of the months, the very first of the months" (Exodus 12:2). The Jewish people's march toward freedom at Passover became the beginning point for Israel's calendar. When you are on a journey, keeping track of time is important. In the year 350 C.E., Hillel II helped to establish a permanent calendar for the Jewish people that coordinated the lunar and solar years with each other.

What you need to know:

1. There are twelve months in the Hebrew calendar. Based on the moon's cycle around the earth, each of them has either 29 or 30 days. Thus, the lunar year is 354 days long.

2. A solar year is 365 days long. In order for the Hebrew lunar months to keep in sync with the earth's annual circuit around the sun, so that the seasons come out at the right time of year, an extra month (Adar II) is added to the Jewish year approximately once every three years.

3. Most people think that the Hebrew calendar numbers the years from the date of the world's creation as determined by Jewish tradition. It's not quite that simple. We recognize the age of the world. However, in ancient times it was customary for events to be dated according to the year of the king's reign. Since we proclaim God as Ruler, we symbolically organize the calendar the same way, reckoning God's "reign" to have begun at the beginning of consciously recorded time.

4. The secular solar calendar counts years from the birth of Jesus, using the abbreviation A.D. (*anno domini*), meaning "in the year of our lord." Thus, 1996 means 1996 years

11

after the birth of Jesus. Dates before the birth of Jesus are followed by the abbreviation B.C.

5. When citing dates in the civil calendar, many Jewish people use the abbreviation C.E. ("common era") instead of A.D., and B.C.E. ("before the common era") instead of B.C.

6. To find a particular date on a Hebrew calendar, simply locate the English date. Most likely, the Hebrew date will appear at the bottom of the box in which the English date appears. For example, the Hebrew date for July 6, 1994, is 27 Tammuz 5754 (see Fig. 2).

7. If you need to find a Hebrew date of many years ago, or if you are interested in learning the Hebrew date of a future year, you can purchase a comprehensive or perpetual Hebrew calendar (see Fig. 1.) There are also Hebrew calendar programs for the computer with which you can project almost any past or future secular date equivalent.

Things to remember:

1. There are twelve lunar months in the Hebrew calendar. Each of them has either 29 or 30 days.

2. The names of the Hebrew months, beginning with the spring month, are Nisan, Iyar, Sivan, Tammuz, Av, Elul, Tishri, Cheshvan, Kislev, Tevet, Shevat, Adar, and, in a leap year, Adar II.

3. There is one leap year (in which an entire month is added) approximately every three years in the Hebrew calendar.

4. The middle of every Hebrew month is a full moon.

5. The Hebrew calendar day begins at sunset.

Key words and phrases:

Adar II אֲדָר ב. Extra month added during leap year in Hebrew calendar.
Chodesh חֹדֶשׁ. Month.
Luach לוּחַ. Calendar.

Rosh Chodesh רֹאשׁ חֹדֶשׁ. New moon, generally the first day of the Hebrew month.

Shanah me'uberet שָׁנָה מְעוּבֶּרֶת. Literally "pregnant year"; a leap year in the Hebrew calendar.

If you want to know more:

Ronald H. Isaacs and Kerry M. Olitzky, *Sacred Celebrations: A Jewish Holiday Handbook* (Hoboken, NJ, 1994).

Arthur Spier, *The Comprehensive Hebrew Calendar* (New York, 1952).

2001 | **5761**

	SUN	MON	TUE	WED	THU	FRI	SAT		SUN	MON	TUE	WED	THU	FRI	SAT	SABBATH	
APRIL	8	9	10	11	12	13	14	⟷	15 Pesah	16 Pesah	17 Hol Hamoed	18 Hol Hamoed	19 Hol Hamoed	20 Hol Hamoed	21 Pesah	Pesah VII	NISAN
	15	16	17	18	19	20	21	⟷	22 Pesah	23	24	25	26	27	28	Shemini*	
	22	23	24	25	26	27	28	⟷	29	30	1	2	3	4	5	Tazria Metzora (0)	IYAR
	29	30	1	2	3	4	5	⟷	6	7	8	9	10	11	12	Ahare Kedoshim (8)	
MAY	6	7	8	9	10	11	12	⟷	13	14	15	16	17	18 Lag Baomer	19	Emor	
	13	14	15	16	17	18	19	⟷	20	21	22	23	24	25	26	Behar* Behukkotai (0)	
	20	21	22	23	24	25	26	⟷	27	28	29	1	2	3	4	Bemidbar	SIVAN
	27	28	29	30	31	1	2	⟷	5	6 Shavuoth	7 Shavuoth	8	9	10	11	Naso	
JUNE	3	4	5	6	7	8	9	⟷	12	13	14	15	16	17	18	Behaalot'cha	
	10	11	12	13	14	15	16	⟷	19	20	21	22	23	24	25	Shelah L'cha*	
	17	18	19	20	21	22	23	⟷	26	27	28	29	30	1	2	Korah	TAMMUZ
	24	25	26	27	28	29	30	⟷	3	4	5	6	7	8	9	Hukkath	
	1	2	3	4	5	6	7	⟷	10	11	12	13	14	15	16	Balak	
JULY	8	9	10	11	12	13	14	⟷	17 Fast Tammuz	18	19	20	21	22	23	Pin'has* (10)	
	15	16	17	18	19	20	21	⟷	24	25	26	27	28	29	1	Mattoth Mase (11, 3)	AB
	22	23	24	25	26	27	28	⟷	2	3	4	5	6	7	8	Devarim Hazon	
	29	30	31	1	2	3	4	⟷	9 Fast Ab	10	11	12	13	14	15	Vaethanan Nahamu	
AUGUST	5	6	7	8	9	10	11	⟷	16	17	18	19	20	21	22	Ekev	
	12	13	14	15	16	17	18	⟷	23	24	25	26	27	28	29	Reeh* (4)	
	19	20	21	22	23	24	25	⟷	30	1	2	3	4	5	6	Shof'tim	
	26	27	28	29	30	31	1	⟷	7	8	9	10	11	12	13	Ki Tetze	ELLUL
SEP	2	3	4	5	6	7	8	⟷	14	15	16	17	18	19	20	Ki Tavo	
	9	10	11	12	13	14	15	⟷	21	22	23	24	25	26	27	Nitzavim	

Reprinted by permission from **The Comprehensive Hebrew Calendar** by Arthur Spier, © 1986. Published by Feldheim Publishers.

Symbols: (0) indicates Haphtarah to be recited. **(1)** through **(12)** indicate special Haphtaroth. Light numerals without designation indicate the days of the New Moon (Rosh Hodesh). *Proclamation of the New Moon (Mevar'chim Hahodesh).

Tishrei–Cheshvan 5756

OCTOBER 1995

תשרי–חשון ה'תשנ"ו

SUNDAY יום ראשון	MONDAY יום שני	TUESDAY יום שלישי	WEDNESDAY יום רביעי	THURSDAY יום חמישי	FRIDAY יום ששי	SATURDAY שבת
1 שמיני עצרת ז'	**2** המוצאי ח'	**3** Kol Nidre יום כפור ט'	**4** Yizkor Yom Kippur יזכור Ends: 7:14 י'	**5** Candles: 6:13 יא'	**6** Candles: 6:13 Ends: 7:14 יב'	**7** הארבעה יג' Ends: 7:14
8 Erev Sukkos ערב סוכות 14 Candles: 6:09 יד'	**9** Columbus Day 1st Day Sukkos יום א' סוכות 15 Candles: 7:11 טו'	**10** 2nd Day Sukkos יום ב' סוכות 16 Ends: 7:09 9:51 סוכ"ש טז'	**11** 1st Day Chol Hamoed שבעות יז' 17 Chol Hamoed	**12** 2nd Day יום ב' 18 Chol Hamoed ח"ו 9:50 סוכ"ש א' יח'	**13** 3rd Day Chol Hamoed המוצא 4th Day Chol Hamoed 19 Candles: 6:01 סוכ"ש יט'	**14** המוצא שבת חול המועד Ends: 7:03 כ'
15 הושענא רבה Hoshanah Rabbah 21 Candles: 5:58 כא'	**16** Yizkor שמיני עצרת יזכור שמחת תורה 16 9:54 סוכ"ש טז' יז'	**17** שמחת תורה Simchas Torah Ends: 6:59 23 9:54 סוכ"ש יז' יח'	**18** אחרי יט' 25	**19** חשון יט' Candles: 5:51 26	**20** חשון כ' Candles: 5:51 Ends: 6:53 27	**21** חשון שבת בראשית Ends: 6:44 כא'
22 Shemini Atzeres שמיני עצרת 22 Candles: 7:00 בא' כב'	**23** Simchas Torah שמחת תורה 1st Day Rosh Chodesh Cheshvan א' דראש חודש 9:58 סוכ"ש כג' כד'	**24** 2nd Day Rosh Chodesh Cheshvan ב' דראש חודש א' חשון 9:58 סוכ"ש 1 כד'	**25** 2nd Day Rosh Chodesh Cheshvan ב' דראש חודש א' חשון 2 25	**26** בראשית כה' 3 26	**27** Candles: 5:41 בראשית כו' ג' 27	**28** חשון שבת בראשית Ends: 6:44 כח' ד' 28
29 Move Back Clock 2 a.m. שבת בראשית ה' 5 6	**30** שבת בראשית ו' 29 30	**31** 9:02 סוכ"ש ז' 31				

Light Candles 18 Minutes Before Sunset

Candle Lighting Time is for New York City Only Daylight Savings Time

When to Say Amen and Mean It
אָמֵן

The source:

The word *amen* (meaning "may it be so") is found in the Torah as an affirmation used in the form of a response. In Deuteronomy 27:15–26, the people respond "Amen" to a series of statements by the Levites. The First Book of Chronicles (16:36), describing an incident during King David's reign (ca. 1000 B.C.E.), reports that the people responded "Amen" when they heard the blessing "Praised be Adonai, God of Israel, from now to all eternity."

What you need to know:

1. When a person says "Amen," he or she is publicly agreeing with what has just been said or endorsing it. It is an affirmation of one's belief.

2. Rabbi Chanina, a talmudic sage, stated that *amen* (אָמֵן) is an acronym for the three Hebrew words *El Melech Ne'eman* (אֵל מֶלֶךְ נֶאֱמָן), meaning "God, Faithful Ruler" (Babylonian Talmud, Shabbat 119b). As such, saying "Amen" acknowledges God as Ruler.

3. Jewish law instructs us to respond "Amen" after we hear another person recite a blessing (Code of Jewish Law, Orach Chayim 215:2 and 124:6).

Things to remember:

1. One never responds "Amen" to a blessing that one says oneself. Amen is only said as a response to a blessing by someone else. Often, this Amen functions as if you had said the blessing and thereby releases you from the obligation of saying it. That's prayer logic.

2. If you are in the midst of saying a prayer that cannot be interrupted, you may not stop even to say "Amen."

3. Never say "Amen" to a blessing that takes God's name in vain.

16

4. When saying "Amen," say it distinctly and in a loud voice (Code of Jewish Law, Orach Chayyim 124:8).

5. Do not say "Amen" for a blessing that you do not actually hear.

Key words and phrases:

Amen אָמֵן. So may it be.

Baruch hu u'varuch shemo בָּרוּךְ הוּא וּבָרוּךְ שְׁמוֹ. Blessed be God and blessed be God's Name (i.e., God's reputation).

Kein yehi ratzon כֵּן יְהִי רָצוֹן. So may it be God's will.

If you want to know more:

Hayim Halevy Donin, *To Pray as a Jew* (New York, 1980).

Sholom Yehuda Gross, *The Amen Response* (New York, 1981).

More particulars:

1. Another prayer response is *Baruch hu u'varuch shemo*, "Blessed be God, and blessed be God's Name." This is the correct response when hearing the (personal) name of God (that is, Adonai), as in the opening part of a blessing, *Baruch atah Adonai* (Code of Jewish Law, Orach Chayyim 124:5).

2. The response to the call to praise God, *Barchu et Adonai hamevorach*, "Praised are You, Source of blessings," is *Baruch Adonai hamevorach l'olam va-ed*, "Praised be Adonai, Source of blessings, throughout all time."

3. The response to each line of the three-sentence Priestly Benediction blessing in the repetition of the *Amidah* prayer is *Kein yehi ratzon*, "So may it be God's will."

4. According to the Babylonian Talmud (Shabbat 119b), the "Amen" response was introduced because some people could not read and therefore could not recite the blessings on their own.

Announcing the New Month
בִּרְכַּת הַחֹדֶשׁ

The source:

During the Rabbinic period, a new month was announced when two independent witnesses reported to the Sanhedrin (rabbinical court) that the crescent of a new moon had appeared. Then an official announcement would be made.

What you need to know:

1. Recite this blessing on the Shabbat before Rosh Chodesh:

יְהִי רָצוֹן מִלְּפָנֶיךָ יהוה אֱלֹהֵינוּ וֵאלֹהֵי אֲבוֹתֵינוּ, שֶׁתְּחַדֵּשׁ עָלֵינוּ אֶת־הַחֹדֶשׁ הַבָּא לְטוֹבָה וְלִבְרָכָה. וְתִתֶּן לָנוּ חַיִּים אֲרֻכִּים, חַיִּים שֶׁל שָׁלוֹם, חַיִּים שֶׁל טוֹבָה, חַיִּים שֶׁל בְּרָכָה, חַיִּים שֶׁל פַּרְנָסָה, חַיִּים שֶׁל חִלּוּץ עֲצָמוֹת, חַיִּים שֶׁיֵּשׁ בָּהֶם יִרְאַת שָׁמַיִם וְיִרְאַת חֵטְא, חַיִּים שֶׁאֵין בָּהֶם בּוּשָׁה וּכְלִמָּה, חַיִּים שֶׁל עֹשֶׁר וְכָבוֹד, חַיִּים שֶׁתְּהֵא בָנוּ אַהֲבַת תּוֹרָה וְיִרְאַת שָׁמַיִם, חַיִּים שֶׁיִּמָּלְאוּ מִשְׁאֲלוֹת לִבֵּנוּ לְטוֹבָה, אָמֵן סֶלָה.

May it be Your will, Adonai our God and God of our ancestors, to renew our lives in the coming month. Grant us a long life, a peaceful life filled with goodness and blessing, sustenance and physical vitality, a life informed by purity and piety, a life free from shame and reproach, a life of abundance and honor, a life encompassing sanctity and love of Torah, a life in which our heart's aspirations for goodness will be fulfilled.

2. Continue with this blessing while holding the Sefer Torah:

מִי שֶׁעָשָׂה נִסִּים לַאֲבוֹתֵינוּ וְגָאַל אוֹתָם מֵעַבְדוּת לְחֵרוּת, הוּא יִגְאַל אוֹתָנוּ בְּקָרוֹב וִיקַבֵּץ נִדָּחֵינוּ מֵאַרְבַּע כַּנְפוֹת הָאָרֶץ, חֲבֵרִים כָּל יִשְׂרָאֵל, וְנֹאמַר אָמֵן.

May the One who brought miracles for our ancestors, moving them from slavery to freedom, redeem us soon and gather our dispersed from the four corners of the earth in the community of the entire people of Israel. And let us say: Amen.

3. While still holding the Sefer Torah, announce the month:

רֹאשׁ חֹדֶשׁ _____ יִהְיֶה בְּיוֹם _____ הַבָּא עָלֵינוּ וְעַל כָּל־יִשְׂרָאֵל לְטוֹבָה.

The new month _____ will begin on _____. May it hold blessings for us and for all the people of Israel.

4. Ask the congregation to repeat the preceding announcement and then continue with its own prayer:

יְחַדְּשֵׁהוּ הַקָּדוֹשׁ בָּרוּךְ הוּא עָלֵינוּ וְעַל כָּל־עַמּוֹ בֵּית יִשְׂרָאֵל לְחַיִּים וּלְשָׁלוֹם, לְשָׂשׂוֹן וּלְשִׂמְחָה, לִישׁוּעָה וּלְנֶחָמָה, וְנֹאמַר אָמֵן.

May the Holy One bless the new month for us and for all Your people, the House of Israel, with life and peace, joy and gladness, deliverance and consolation. And let us say: Amen.

5. Then repeat the prayer just said by the congregation.

Things to remember:

While we are able to calculate the arrival of a new moon (and therefore the Reform movement only marks one day of Rosh Chodesh), we still announce the coming of the new month in the synagogue on the Shabbat before it begins.

1. This procedure for announcing the month is followed for each month, except for Tishri. Because Rosh Hashanah begins on the first of Tishri, it is unnecessary to do so.

Key words and phrases:

Rosh Chodesh רֹאשׁ חֹדֶשׁ. New month.
Shabbat Mevarchim שַׁבָּת מְבָרְכִים. Shabbat on which the prayer for the new moon is recited.

If you want to know more:

Hayim Halevy Donin, *To Pray as a Jew* (New York, 1980).
Chaim Lipschutz, *Kiddush Levono: The Monthly Blessing of the Moon* (Brooklyn, 1987).
Abraham Millgram, *Jewish Worship* (Philadelphia, 1971).

More particulars:

1. The cycle of the moon is approximately 29 days. However, some months in the Hebrew calendar are 30 days. Therefore, Rosh Chodesh is often celebrated on two days, once on the 29th day of the cycle (which may be marked as the 30th day of a particular month) and on the first day of the month whether it coincides with the cycle or is simply the first day of the month.

2. When announcing the new month, some cantors will use a melody that somehow reflects the month about to be celebrated. For example, when announcing the new month of Kislev in which Chanukkah is celebrated, many cantors use the melody for "Maoz Tzur."

Blessing the Sun
בִּרְכַּת הַחַמָּה

The source:

Our rabbis taught that a person who sees the sun at its turning point, the moon in its power, the planets in their orbits, or the signs of the zodiac in their order should say: "Praised are You who makes the work of creation." When does this occur? Abaye said, "Every twenty-eight years, when the cycle begins again and the spring equinox falls in Saturn on the evening of Tuesday, going into Wednesday" (Babylonian Talmud, Berachot 59b).

What you need to know:

1. The blessing of the sun is a prayer service in which the sun is blessed in thanksgiving for its creation and its being set into motion in the firmament on the fourth day of creation (see Genesis 1:16–19).

2. The ceremony of the blessing of the sun takes place once every twenty-eight years. It takes place after the morning service, when the sun is about 90 degrees above the eastern horizon, on the first Wednesday of the month of Nisan (late March–early April).

3. When you see the sun on the morning following the vernal equinox, begin your service by reciting Psalms 84:12, 72:5; 75:2, Malachi 3:20, Psalm 97:6, and Psalm 148. Then recite this blessing:

בָּרוּךְ אַתָּה יהוה אֱלֹהֵינוּ מֶלֶךְ הָעוֹלָם, עוֹשֶׂה מַעֲשֵׂה בְרֵאשִׁית.

Baruch atah Adonai elohaynu melech ha'olam oseh ma'asey v'reshit.

Praised are You, Adonai our God, Sovereign of the Universe, Source of creation.

Next read Psalms 19 and 121, the hymn *El Adon,* and the Talmud passage quoted above. The ritual ends

21

with a thanksgiving prayer in which the community says thank you to God for sustaining it.

Things to remember:

1. Although it is preferable to recite the blessing in the midst of a community (minimally with a *minyan*), even traditional Jewish law does not require this.

2. The blessing of the sun should be recited while standing. It should be pronounced as early in the day as possible.

3. The blessing is usually not recited if the sun is obscured by clouds.

Key words and phrases:

Chamah חַמָּה. Sun.

If you want to know more:

Encyclopaedia Judaica (Jerusalem, 1971), 15:518.
J. David Bleich, *Bircas HaChammah* (New York, 1980).

More particulars:

During the latter half of the twentieth century, the community blessed the sun on April 8, 1953 and March 18, 1981. The blessing of the sun will next occur on April 7, 2009.

Blessing the Moon
קִדּוּשׁ לְבָנָה

The source:

The blessing of the moon originated in the time of the Second Temple. The basic text for blessing the moon is presented in the Talmud (Sanhedrin 42a and Soferim 2:1). However, you will find many subsequent additions in the blessing used today.

What you need to know:

1. The blessing of the moon, known in Hebrew as *birkat ha'levanah* or *kiddush levanah* (sanctification of the moon), is a prayer of thanksgiving recited at the periodical reappearance of the moon's crescent.

2. The prayer can be recited from the third evening after the appearance of the new moon until the fifteenth of the lunar month. After that day, the moon begins to diminish.

3. We suggest that you recite the blessing of the moon on Saturday night, following the departure of the Sabbath, when you are still in a festive mood and dressed in your festive clothes.

4. We recite the blessing of the new moon because we understand the moon as a symbol of the renewal of nature as well as of Israel's renewal and redemption. Here is the basic text for blessing the new moon:

אָמַר רַבִּי יוֹחָנָן: כָּל־הַמְבָרֵךְ אֶת־הַחֹדֶשׁ בִּזְמַנּוֹ כְּאִלּוּ מְקַבֵּל פְּנֵי הַשְּׁכִינָה:
הַלְלוּיָהּ הַלְלוּ אֶת־יהוה מִן הַשָּׁמַיִם הַלְלוּהוּ בַּמְּרוֹמִים: הַלְלוּהוּ כָל־מַלְאָכָיו הַלְלוּהוּ כָּל־צְבָאָיו: הַלְלוּהוּ שֶׁמֶשׁ וְיָרֵחַ הַלְלוּהוּ כָּל־כּוֹכְבֵי אוֹר: הַלְלוּהוּ שְׁמֵי הַשָּׁמָיִם וְהַמַּיִם אֲשֶׁר מֵעַל הַשָּׁמָיִם: יְהַלְלוּ אֶת־שֵׁם יהוה כִּי הוּא צִוָּה וְנִבְרָאוּ: וַיַּעֲמִידֵם לָעַד לְעוֹלָם חָק־נָתַן וְלֹא יַעֲבוֹר:
בָּרוּךְ אַתָּה יהוה אֱלֹהֵינוּ מֶלֶךְ הָעוֹלָם אֲשֶׁר בְּמַאֲמָרוֹ בָּרָא שְׁחָקִים וּבְרוּחַ פִּיו כָּל־צְבָאָם. חֹק וּזְמַן נָתַן לָהֶם שֶׁלֹּא יְשַׁנּוּ

אֶת־תַּפְקִידָם. שָׂשִׂים וּשְׂמֵחִים לַעֲשׂוֹת רְצוֹן קוֹנָם. פּוֹעֵל אֱמֶת שֶׁפְּעֻלָּתוֹ אֱמֶת. וְלַלְּבָנָה אָמַר שֶׁתִּתְחַדֵּשׁ עֲטֶרֶת תִּפְאֶרֶת לַעֲ־ מוּסֵי בָטֶן. שֶׁהֵם עֲתִידִים לְהִתְחַדֵּשׁ כְּמוֹתָהּ וּלְפָאֵר לְיוֹצְרָם עַל שֵׁם כְּבוֹד מַלְכוּתוֹ: בָּרוּךְ אַתָּה יהוה, מְחַדֵּשׁ חֳדָשִׁים:

Rabbi Yochanan said: "Whoever blesses the new moon at the proper time is considered as having welcomed the presence of the *Shechinah*."

Halleluyah. Praise Adonai from the heavens. Praise God, angels on High. Praise God, sun and moon and shining stars. Praise God, highest heavens. Let them praise the glory of Adonai at whose command they were created, at whose command they endure forever, and by whose laws nature abides. (Psalm 148:1–6)

Praised are You, Adonai our God, Sovereign of the Universe, whose word created the heavens, whose breath created all that they contain. God set statutes and seasons for them, that they should not deviate from their assigned task. Happily they do the will of their Creator, whose work is dependable. God spoke to the moon: renew yourself, crown of glory for those who were borne in the womb, who also are destined to be renewed and to extol their Creator for God's glorious sovereignty. Praised are You, Adonai, who renews the months.

דָּוִד מֶלֶךְ יִשְׂרָאֵל חַי וְקַיָּם:

King David of Israel lives and endures.
Greetings are exchanged:
Shalom Aleichem   שָׁלוֹם עֲלֵיכֶם
Aleichem Shalom   עֲלֵיכֶם שָׁלוֹם

סִמָּן טוֹב וּמַזָּל טוֹב יִהְיֶה לָנוּ וּלְכָל יִשְׂרָאֵל. אָמֵן:

May good fortune be ours and blessing for the entire House of Israel. Amen.

Things to remember:

1. It is preferable to recite the blessing of the new moon with a *minyan* (prayer quorum of ten persons).

2. The blessing of the new moon is recited only if the moon is clearly visible (in other words, not hidden by clouds). It should preferably be said outdoors in open space.

3. In some communities, the blessing of the new moon in the month of Av is delayed until after Tisha B'Av, in Tishri until after the Day of Atonement, and in Tevet until after the fast of the Tenth of Tevet.

4. A mourner should not recite the blessing for the moon until after *shivah* (the week of mourning) is concluded.

5. The blessing of the new moon is traditionally not recited on Sabbath evenings because of the traditional prohibition against carrying prayer books outside the house or synagogue.

Key words and phrases:

Birkat Levanah בִּרְכַּת לְבָנָה. Blessing of the new moon.

Kiddush Levanah קִדּוּשׁ לְבָנָה. Sanctification of the new moon, another way of saying: blessing of the new moon.

Shalom Aleichem שָׁלוֹם עֲלֵיכֶם. Traditional form of greeting, literally, "Peace be unto you."

Siman tov u'mazel tov סִמָן טוֹב וּמַזָּל טוֹב. May you have good fortune and good luck.

If you want to know more:

Philip Birnbaum, *A Book of Jewish Concepts* (New York, 1964).

Joseph Hertz, *Daily Prayer Book* (New York, 1961).

Elie Munk, *The World of Prayer* (New York, 1963), vol. 2, pp. 94–101.

More particulars:

1. The expression "Long live King David of Israel" refers to Psalm 89:38, which says that David's dynasty shall "like the moon be established forever." The numerical value of *David melech yisrael chai vekayam* (819) is equal to the numerical equivalent of *rosh chodesh* (new month). As a

result, the phrase *rosh chodesh* became the password of Bar Kochba's army!

2. According to mystical tradition, a worshipper who says *siman tov* should perform three dancing gestures in the direction of the moon while saying three times: "Just as I cannot touch you, may my enemies never be able to harm me."

Entertaining Bride and Groom
מְשַׂמֵּחַ חָתָן וְכַלָּה

The source:

In the *Mishneh Torah* of Maimonides (Avelim 14:1), the rabbis instruct us to rejoice with the bride and groom at a wedding.

What you need to know:

1. In ancient times the betrothal and the marriage were separate ceremonies often weeks or months apart. Since the modern wedding combines the betrothal with the marriage, two cups of wine are used in the ceremony.

2. Witnesses may sign the *ketubah* (marriage document) in private before the ceremony but must be present during the ceremony. They must not be blood relatives of the bride or groom or of one another.

3. Following the reading of the *ketubah,* the officiant reads or chants these seven blessings:

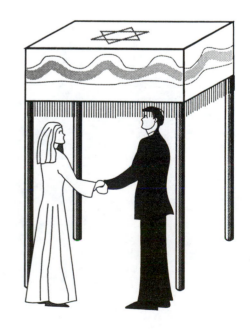

בָּרוּךְ אַתָּה יהוה אֱלֹהֵינוּ מֶלֶךְ הָעוֹלָם, בּוֹרֵא פְּרִי הַגָּפֶן:

בָּרוּךְ אַתָּה יהוה אֱלֹהֵינוּ מֶלֶךְ הָעוֹלָם, שֶׁהַכֹּל בָּרָא לִכְבוֹדוֹ:

בָּרוּךְ אַתָּה יהוה אֱלֹהֵינוּ מֶלֶךְ הָעוֹלָם, יוֹצֵר הָאָדָם:

בָּרוּךְ אַתָּה יהוה אֱלֹהֵינוּ מֶלֶךְ הָעוֹלָם, אֲשֶׁר יָצַר אֶת הָאָדָם בְּצַלְמוֹ, בְּצֶלֶם דְּמוּת תַּבְנִיתוֹ, וְהִתְקִין לוֹ מִמֶּנּוּ בִּנְיַן עֲדֵי עַד, בָּרוּךְ אַתָּה יהוה, יוֹצֵר הָאָדָם:

שׂוֹשׂ תָּשִׂישׂ וְתָגֵל הָעֲקָרָה, בְּקִבּוּץ בָּנֶיהָ לְתוֹכָהּ בְּשִׂמְחָה, בָּרוּךְ אַתָּה יהוה, מְשַׂמֵּחַ צִיּוֹן בְּבָנֶיהָ:

שַׂמֵּחַ תְּשַׂמַּח רֵעִים הָאֲהוּבִים, כְּשַׂמֵּחֲךָ יְצִירְךָ בְּגַן עֵדֶן מִקֶּדֶם, בָּרוּךְ אַתָּה יהוה, מְשַׂמֵּחַ חָתָן וְכַלָּה:

בָּרוּךְ אַתָּה יהוה אֱלֹהֵינוּ מֶלֶךְ הָעוֹלָם, אֲשֶׁר בָּרָא שָׂשׂוֹן וְשִׂמְחָה, חָתָן וְכַלָּה, גִּילָה רִנָּה, דִּיצָה וְחֶדְוָה, אַהֲבָה וְאַחֲוָה, וְשָׁלוֹם וְרֵעוּת, מְהֵרָה יהוה אֱלֹהֵינוּ יִשָּׁמַע בְּעָרֵי יְהוּדָה וּבְחוּצוֹת יְרוּשָׁלָיִם, קוֹל שָׂשׂוֹן, וְקוֹל שִׂמְחָה, קוֹל חָתָן וְקוֹל כַּלָּה, קוֹל מִצְהֲלוֹת חֲתָנִים מֵחֻפָּתָם, וּנְעָרִים מִמִּשְׁתֵּה נְגִינָתָם, בָּרוּךְ אַתָּה יהוה, מְשַׂמֵּחַ חָתָן עִם הַכַּלָּה:

27

Praised are You, Adonai our God, Sovereign of the Universe, who creates the fruit of the vine.

Praised are You, Adonai our God, Sovereign of the Universe, who has created all things to Your glory.

Praised are You, Adonai our God, Sovereign of the Universe, who has made the human species.

Praised are You, Adonai our God, Sovereign of the Universe, who has made the human in Your image, after Your likeness, and has prepared for each human a perpetual fabric out of his/her essential self. Praised are You, Adonai, Creator of the human species.

May Zion who was barren be exceptionally glad and rejoice when her children joyfully gather around her. Praised are You, Adonai, who makes Zion joyful through her children.

Oh make these loving companions rejoice greatly, just as You gladdened the creatures in the Garden of Eden. Praised are You, who makes brides and grooms rejoice.

Praised are You, Adonai our God, Sovereign of the Universe, who has created joy and gladness, bride and groom, mirth and exultation, pleasure and delight, harmony, peace, and fellowship. Soon may there be heard in the cities of Judah, and in the streets of Jerusalem, the voice of joy and gladness, the voice of the groom and the bride, the jubilant voice of lovers from their *chuppot,* and youth from their feasts of song. Praised are You, Adonai our God, who causes brides and grooms to rejoice.

4. Now the groom breaks the glass and everyone shouts, *Mazel tov!*

Things to remember:

1. According to Jewish law, marital status can be attained through one of three acts: (1) before witnesses (i.e., a marriage ceremony); (2) through cohabitation before witnesses (technically legal but considered immoral); (3) through the delivery of a written document [betrothed] from a man to a woman or the presentation of a valuable article [wedding] by the man to the woman. Today's wedding represents the ceremonial enactment of these three

actions, combining the betrothal and wedding together in one formal ceremony.

2. According to tradition, "Even the study of Torah may be suspended to rejoice with bride and groom" (Babylonian Talmud, Ketuvot 17b).

3. The bride always stands to the right of the groom (see Psalm 45:10 for the textual reference).

4. Traditionally, marriages are celebrated for seven days. The *shevah berachot* are recited each day at a festive meal.

5. If their parents are dead, the bride and groom should visit their graves before the wedding to recite *El Maleh Rachamin* and pray for happiness in their marriage.

6. The preparations for a marriage often include a visit to the *mikvah* (ritual bath).

Key words and phrases:

Aufruf (Yiddish) אָפְרוּף. Literally "calling up"; refers to the Torah *aliyah* prior to one's wedding.

Badeken (Yiddish) בַּאדֶעקֶן. The ceremonial covering of the bride's face before the marriage ceremony, derived from Rebecca's covering herself with a veil before meeting Isaac (see Genesis 24:65).

Chuppah חוּפָּה. Marriage canopy, from "to cover with garlands."

Hachnasat kallah הַכְנָסַת כַּלָה. Bringing in the bride.

Ketubah כְּתֻבָּה. Marriage contract.

Kiddushin קִדּוּשִׁין. Literally "holy and separate," referring to marriage, alternatively called *nissuin* נְשׂוּאִין.

Kinyan sudor קִנְיָן סוּדָר. Agreement by handkerchief.

Nissuin נְשׂוּאִין. Wedding or marriage, alternatively called *kiddushin*.

Shadchan שַׁדְכָן. Matchmaker.

Sheva berachot שֶׁבַע בְּרָכוֹת. Seven wedding blessings.

Shidduch שִׁדּוּךְ. Literally "connection"; refers to establishing a connection between people for the purpose of marriage.

Tenaim תְּנָאִים. Conditions for the marriage.

Yichud יִחוּד. Act of consummation (i.e., unchaperoned togetherness).

If you want to know more:

Anita Diament, *The New Jewish Wedding* (New York, 1985).

Philip and Hanna Goodman, *The Jewish Marriage Anthology* (Philadelphia, 1965).

Ronald H. Isaacs, *The Bride and Groom Handbook* (West Orange, NJ, 1987).

—— and Leora W. Isaacs, *Loving Companions: Our Jewish Wedding Album* (Northvale, NJ, 1991).

More particulars:

1. It is the custom not to marry a woman bearing the same first name as one's mother.

2. Biblically, *kohanim* (priestly descendants) are not permitted to marry divorced women or converts. Reform rabbis and many Conservative and Reconstructionist rabbis reject this prohibition.

3. Bride and groom are often showered with nuts by the wedding guests since the alphanumerical equivalent of *egoz* ("nuts") is equal to *tov* ("good") in gematria. Another custom includes the throwing of raisins and candies. Rice and nuts are symbols of fertility.

4. Often, a bride will present a groom with a *tallit* prior to the wedding because the verse in Torah which refers to *tzitzit* comes right before the verse about a man and woman marrying (Deuteronomy 12:12).

5. Tuesday is a favorite day for weddings because the Torah uses the phrase *ki tov*, "And it was good," twice in its account of the third day of creation.

6. There are several periods in the calendar during which time marriages are traditionally prohibited. Check with the local rabbi for the custom of the community. In particular, weddings do not take place between Pesach and Lag B'omer or between Rosh Chodesh Iyar and Shavuot. Likewise, they are not scheduled for the three weeks prior to Tisha B'Av. Some Reform and Reconstructionist rabbis interpret these prohibitions more liberally. While there is no prohibition against marrying between Rosh Hashanah and Yom Kippur, people tend to avoid having weddings during this intense period of introspection.

7. Traditionally, bride and groom fast on their wedding day in order to ask forgiveness as they enter upon their new life together. The Talmud assures the couple that the act of getting married provides atonement for previous transgressions.

8. The groom's *tallit* is often used as a *chuppah* because it represents the commitment of one to protect the other.

Doing Gematria
גִּימַטְרִיָּה

The source:

Gematria, or numerology, is a device used to interpret the Torah. It is one of the thirty-two methods of interpreting the Bible permitted by the rabbis.

What you need to know:

1. Gematria is a method used to discover the hidden meaning of Torah texts and other texts by manipulating the numerical equivalents of the Hebrew letters in particular words.

2. At times, gematria is used as a playful number game. Mystical literature has made much use of speculations based on the numerical values of the Hebrew letters. For example, since the word *torah* (תּוֹרָה) has the numerical value of 611, it refers to the 611 commandments transmitted to Israel through Moses, which together with the first two commandments of the Ten Commandments given directly to Israel by God on Mount Sinai make up the 613 positive and negative precepts.

Another example: The numerical value of the word אֶחָד (one) is the same as that of אַהֲבָה (love). This teaches us that the highest goal we should try to attain is love for God, who is One.

3. There are a variety of systems of gematria. *Atbash* refers to the one wherein the last letter of the alphabet, ת (*tav*), is substituted for the first letter, א (*alef*); the next-to-last, ש (*shin*), is substituted for the second, (*bet*); and so forth. This method is quite ancient, as shown by its use in Jeremiah 51:1.

Things to remember:

1. When doing gematria you will need to know the numerical values of the Hebrew letters. Here is a handy reference for you to use:

100	ק	40	מ	7	ז	1	א
200	ר	50	נ	8	ח	2	ב
300	ש	60	ס	9	ט	3	ג
400	ת	70	ע	10	י	4	ד
		80	פ	20	כ	5	ה
		90	צ	30	ל	6	ו

2. Gematria has little significance in Jewish law, but occupies an important place in the rich treasury of rabbinic literature interpreting the Bible.

3. One of the most well-known numbers in gematria is 18, which is equivalent to the Hebrew word *chai* (חַי), meaning "life." When giving *tzedakah*, it is customary to give amounts in multiples of 18, such as 36, 72, and so forth.

Key words and phrases:

Atbash אַתְבַּשׁ. System of gematria which consists of substituting the last letter of the Hebrew alphabet ת for the first א, and so forth.

If you want to know more:

Philip Birnbaum, *A Jewish Book of Concepts* (New York, 1964).
Encyclopaedia Judaica (Jerusalem, 1973), 7:369–374.

More particulars:

While this system is rarely used, there is a method of gematria in which the letters of the words are calculated according to their squared numerical value. Thus, for example, יהוה (Adonai), a name of God, $= 10^2 + 5^2 + 6^2 + 5^2 = 186 =$ מָקוֹם ("Place"), another name for God.

Making a *Misheberach*
מִי שֶׁבֵּרַךְ

The source:

Misheberach is a collapsed form (that's a technical term) of the two words *Mi sheberach,* "the One who blesses," namely God. Thus, when we speak of "making a *misheberach*," we are referring to a prayer asking God to bless a particular person or persons with well-being, especially in the case of prayers for healing or celebration (such as a Bar/Bat Mitzvah).

What you need to know:

1. While *Misheberach* prayers can be said at any time for nearly any purpose, they are generally said in public, during the Torah service, following a concluding Torah blessing.

2. Anyone can say a *Misheberach* blessing; you don't have to be a rabbi or a cantor, just a Jew who believes in the efficacy of prayer.

3. These blessings generally are said to bless the congregation, individuals who are ill, those called up for Torah honors, those celebrating a Bar or Bat Mitzvah, and people preparing for marriage.

4. Here is the basic text for one who is called to the Torah:

מִי שֶׁבֵּרַךְ אֲבוֹתֵינוּ אַבְרָהָם יִצְחָק וְיַעֲקֹב, הוּא יְבָרֵךְ אֶת
(פלוני בן פלוני) בַּעֲבוּר שֶׁעָלָה לִכְבוֹד הַמָּקוֹם, לִכְבוֹד הַתּוֹרָה,
(בשבת לִכְבוֹד הַשַּׁבָּת,) (ביום טוב לִכְבוֹד הָרֶגֶל,) בִּשְׂכַר זֶה,
הַקָּדוֹשׁ בָּרוּךְ הוּא יִשְׁמְרֵהוּ וְיַצִּילֵהוּ מִכָּל צָרָה וְצוּקָה, וּמִכָּל
נֶגַע וּמַחֲלָה, וְיִשְׁלַח בְּרָכָה וְהַצְלָחָה בְּכָל מַעֲשֵׂה יָדָיו, (ביום
טוב וְיִזְכֶּה לַעֲלוֹת לָרֶגֶל,) עִם כָּל יִשְׂרָאֵל אֶחָיו, וְנֹאמַר אָמֵן:

May the One who blessed our ancestors Abraham, Isaac, and Jacob, Sarah, Rebecca, Leah, and Rachel, bless _____ who has come for an *aliyah* with reverence for God and respect for the Torah. May the Holy One bless him/her and his/her family and cause to succeed all that he/she does, together with the deeds of fellow Jews everywhere. And let us say: Amen.

5. Here is the basic text for one who is ill:

מִי שֶׁבֵּרַךְ אֲבוֹתֵינוּ אַבְרָהָם יִצְחָק וְיַעֲקֹב, מֹשֶׁה אַהֲרֹן דָּוִד וּשְׁלֹמֹה, הוּא יְבָרֵךְ וִירַפֵּא אֶת הַחוֹלֶה (פלוני בן פלונית) בַּעֲבוּר שֶׁ(פלוני בן פלוני) יִתֵּן לִצְדָקָה בַּעֲבוּרוֹ. בִּשְׂכַר זֶה, הַקָּדוֹשׁ בָּרוּךְ הוּא יִמָּלֵא רַחֲמִים עָלָיו, לְהַחֲלִימוֹ וּלְרַפֹּאתוֹ וּלְהַחֲזִיקוֹ וּלְהַחֲיוֹתוֹ, וְיִשְׁלַח לוֹ מְהֵרָה רְפוּאָה שְׁלֵמָה מִן הַשָּׁמַיִם, לִרְמַ"ח אֵבָרָיו, וּשְׁסָ"ה גִּידָיו, בְּתוֹךְ שְׁאָר חוֹלֵי יִשְׂרָאֵל, רְפוּאַת הַנֶּפֶשׁ, וּרְפוּאַת הַגּוּף, (בשבת שַׁבָּת הִיא מִלִּזְעֹק, וּרְפוּאָה קְרוֹבָה לָבֹא,) (ביום טוב יוֹם טוֹב הוּא מִלִּזְעֹק, וּרְפוּאָה קְרוֹבָה לָבֹא,) הַשְׁתָּא, בַּעֲגָלָא וּבִזְמַן קָרִיב, וְנֹאמַר אָמֵן:

May the One who blessed our ancestors Abraham, Isaac, and Jacob, Sarah, Rebecca, Leah, and Rachel, bless and heal _____. May the Holy One in mercy strengthen him/her and heal him/her soon, body and soul, together with all others who suffer from illness. And let us say: Amen.

Things to remember:

1. In some congregations, collective prayers for healing are offered. In other synagogues, entire services are devoted to prayers of healing.

2. If the Torah scroll is still open on the reader's desk, as it should be, while the *Misheberach* is being said, place the Torah mantle (*me'il*) over the Torah during the prayer. (Don't re-dress the Torah.) Some congregations have an additional cover to be used for this purpose.

3. When using a person's Hebrew name, there are two different customs regarding the *Misheberach* prayer. If it is a prayer to honor someone, then the person is called in the name of his or her father. When the prayer is for healing, the individual is called in the name of his or her mother. In this age of political correctness, decide for

yourself, but remember to check on the *minhag ha'makom* (the custom of the place).

Key words and phrases:

Aliyah עֲלִיָה. Literally, "going up" or "ascending"; a Torah honor.
Berachah בְּרָכָה. Blessing.

If you want to know more:

Jules Harlow, *A Rabbi's Manual* (New York, 1965).
David Polish, *Rabbi's Manual* (New York, 1988).

A Parent's Prayer for Bar/Bat Mitzvah

בַּר/בַּת מִצְוָה

The source:

"At thirteen, one is ready for *mitzvot*" (Avot 5:2).

What you need to know:

1. When the parents of a Bar/Bat Mitzvah child are called to the Torah to recite the Torah blessing, they traditionally add, *Baruch she-petarani me'ansho shel zeh,* "Praised is the One who has freed me from the responsibility for this child's actions." Traditionally this was spoken by the father of the Bar Mitzvah as the son concluded reciting the Torah blessings.

2. As an alternative, try this blessing (or, better yet, just speak from the heart):
Into our hands, O God, You have placed Your Torah, to be held high by parents and children, and taught by one generation to the next. Whatever has befallen us, our people have remained steadfast in loyalty to the Torah. It was carried into exile in the arms of parents that their children might not be deprived of their birthright. And now I pray that you, my child, will always be worthy of this inheritance. Take its teaching into your heart, and in turn, pass it on to your children and those who come after you. May you be a faithful Jew, searching for wisdom and truth, working justice and peace. Thus will you be among those who labor to bring nearer the day when Adonai shall be One and God's name shall be One.

—Adapted from *Gates of Prayer*

Things to remember:

1. A Bar or Bat Mitzvah may take place on any day when the Torah is read at services, including Mondays, Thursdays, and Rosh Chodesh (the first day/days of the month).

2. When one becomes a Bar/Bat Mitzvah and from that day forward, one takes personal responsibility for one's religious conduct.

3. Whether the occasion is marked with a ceremony or not, a child becomes Bar or Bat Mitzvah (i.e., personally responsible from the standpoint of Jewish law) at thirteen (some maintain the traditional age for girls of twelve years plus one day).

Key words and phrases:

Grammen גראַמֶן. Rhymed lyrics about the Bar or Bat Mitzvah child.

If you want to know more:

Jeffrey Salkin, *Putting God on the Guest List: How to Reclaim the Spiritual Meaning of Your Child's Bar or Bat Mitzvah* (Woodstock, VT, 1992).

More particulars:

1. Some parents follow the custom of taking the *tallit* from their own shoulders and placing it on the shoulders of their child prior to reading the Torah blessings.

2. Often these blessings are preceded by what has come to be known as the Torah transmission ceremony in which an elder of the family hands the Torah scroll to the Bar/Bat Mitzvah, thereby symbolically passing the Torah from one generation to the next.

3. The Torah transmission ceremony sometimes takes place when the Torah scroll is taken from the ark, the elder removing it and handing it on to the youngster.

4. The parental blessing is sometimes concluded by reciting the *Shehecheyanu*. In some congregations, the Torah transmission ceremony replaces the parental blessing.

How to Make a Blessing or Say a Prayer
בְּרָכָה

The source:

Babylonian Talmud, Tractate Berachot.

What you need to know:

1. Blessings are simple. Begin with the traditional formula. It is probably well known to you. Here is the phrase that begins most blessings: *Baruch atah Adonai elohaynu melech ha'olam,* "Praised are You, Adonai our God, Sovereign of the Universe."

2. Then continue with the subject of your blessing, whatever is on your mind: peace, love, health, your children.

3. Prayers are just a little more complex. Here's how they work.
There are three simple sections to any prayer:

    a. The introductory *berachah,* which establishes the theme of the prayer.
    b. The middle part of the prayer, which gives the details.
    c. The closing *berachah,* which recaps the theme of the prayer.

Things to remember:

1. Anyone can offer a blessing. You don't have to be a rabbi.

2. Making blessings is serious business. By making a blessing, you are inviting God's presence—and God's power—into your midst.

3. We use traditional formulas for blessings because they ensure that our prayer statements are in harmony with the principles of the Judaic heritage. Often we feel unpoetic and turn to the tradition for spiritual insight, especially

on designated occasions of blessing. However, feel free to transcend the traditional parameters and offer your own prayer.

Key words and phrases:

Berachah בְּרָכָה. Blessing.

Iyyun tefillah עִיּוּן תְּפִלָּה. Transcending the words of the prayer by capturing its spiritual essence.

Kavannah כַּוָּנָה. The intention or attitude with which one prays, one's spiritual posture.

Kevah קֶבַע. Fixed prayer.

Klalah קְלָלָה. Opposite of blessing; curse.

M'ayrah מְאָרָה. Opposite of blessing; curse.

Tefillah תְּפִלָּה. Prayer.

If you want to know more:

Joel Lurie Grishaver, *And You Shall Be a Blessing: An Unfolding of the Six Words That Begin Every Brakhah* (Northvale, NJ, 1993).

More particulars:

1. Some people are uncomfortable with the traditional language of blessing and prefer to change the Hebrew or its English translation. In many instances this is to ensure that the language referring to worshippers, both individual and collectively, and/or to the Jewish people is gender-sensitive or gender-neutral. In addition, some feel that male images of God (like *melech ha'olam,* "King of the World") need to be changed (for example, to *mekor chayim,* "Source of Life"). Do what is comfortable for you and your community.

2. Say the *Shehecheyanu* blessing whenever you experience something new:

בָּרוּךְ אַתָּה יהוה אֱלֹהֵינוּ מֶלֶךְ הָעוֹלָם, שֶׁהֶחֱיָנוּ וְקִיְּמָנוּ וְהִגִּיעָנוּ, לַזְּמַן הַזֶּה:

Baruch atah Adonai elohaynu melech ha'olam she-hecheyanu ve'keemanu ve'heegeeyanu lazman ha'zeh.

Praised are You, Adonai our God, Sovereign of the Universe, who has kept us alive, sustained us, and enabled us to reach this day.

Saying *Selichot*
סְלִיחוֹת

The source:

"At midnight, I will rise to give thanks to You" (Psalm 119:62).

What you need to know:

Selichot services are held at midnight on the Saturday night prior to Rosh Hashanah unless Rosh Hashanah falls shortly thereafter (on Monday or Tuesday). In that case, *Selichot* are held on the preceding Saturday.

Things to remember:

1. Special *Selichot* services are scheduled during fast days, on occasions requesting God's intercession, and during the period between Rosh Hashanah and Yom Kippur.

2. Sephardim begin saying *Selichot* prayers forty days before Rosh Hashanah and continue through Yom Kippur, while Ashkenazim begin on the Saturday night (at midnight) before Rosh Hashanah and continue through Yom Kippur.

3. Originally the *Selichot* prayers were offered after the sixth blessing of the *Amidah*. Generally, they are now offered after the entire *Amidah*.

4. *Selichot* are also said on semi-official fast days—depending on the tradition of the community—like the Monday, Thursday, and Monday after Passover and Sukkot; in leap years on the Thursday before each of the eight Sabbaths when reading the Torah portions *Shemot* through *Tetzaveh;* on Yom Kippur Katan by members of the Chevra Kaddisha; and, according to Jewish tradition, to avert plagues affecting children.

Key words and phrases:

Selichot סְלִיחוֹת (singular, *selichah* סְלִיחָה). The singular form refers to individual *piyutim* (liturgical poems) whose subject is the forgiveness of sins; the plural

41

form designates a special order of service consisting of nonstatutory additional prayers for the forgiveness of sins recited during various penitential periods.

If you want to know more:

Rachel Adler and Yaffa Weisman, *Selihot Service* (Los Angeles, 1991).

Gates of Forgiveness (New York, 1980).

Sidney Greenberg, *Contemporary Prayers and Readings for the High Holidays, Sabbaths and Special Occasions* (Bridgeport, CT, 1974).

Harold Kushner, *New Prayers for the High Holy Days* (Bridgeport, CT, 1973).

Jack Reimer, *The World of the High Holidays: Poems, Parables, Prayers, Stories, Insights and Words of Torah for the Days of Awe* (Miami, FL, 1992).

Starting a Jewish Library at Home
סִפְרִיָּה

The source:

"Talmud Torah is more important than other *mitzvot* [of unlimited quantity] because it leads to them all" (Peah 1:1).

What you need to know:

There are lots of books you can purchase to start a home Jewish library. As Kohelet said, "Of the making of books there is no end" (Ecclesiastes 12:12). Here are some categories to begin with:

1. Bible

> a. A Hebrew Bible with a readable English translation.
> b. A commentary on the weekly Torah portions. Linear commentaries, as they are called, help you to follow the English translation while improving your Hebrew skills at the same time. Remember to get one that fits into the way you view the Jewish world—or the way you would like to view it. Remember to use a *Chumash* so that you can follow the weekly Torah reading. There are many books which offer a specific prism through which to read the weekly portion (like *Sparks Beneath the Surface: A Spiritual Commentary on the Torah* by Lawrence Kushner and Kerry Olitzky).

2. Prayer book
In addition to your own *siddur,* the one you use regularly, keep on hand the standard prayer books of other movements and perhaps a few examples of prayerbooks prepared by congregations for their own use.

3. Encyclopedia
The *Encyclopaedia Judaica* has become the standard. Remember to buy the yearbooks to keep it up to date. However, there are some excellent one-volume reference books. Try *A Glossary of Jewish Life* by Ron Isaacs and

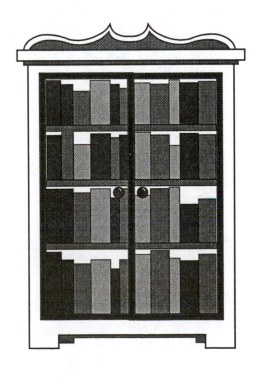

Kerry Olitzky or the new *Oxford Dictionary of Jewish Religion* edited by Geoffrey Wigoder. Other encyclopedias have different emphases. For example, the out-of-print *Universal Jewish Encyclopedia* is excellent for pre-1940 Jewish Americana. Used-book stores are great resources for out-of-print classics like the *UJE*.

4. History

All historians (and therefore all history books) interpret history according to their own understanding of it. Therefore, when you acquire a history book, try to get a sense of the historian's point-of-view ahead of time. Book jackets are great sources for this approach. Some books are written simply in order to present a theoretical construction of Jewish history, like *The Shaping of Jewish History* by Ellis Rivkin. We like to recommend complementary (or synthetic, if you prefer) viewpoints. For example, *A Certain People* by Charles Silberman and *The Jews in America* by Arthur Hertzberg present a balanced look at the current state of the North American Jewish community. Make sure you have a good set of volumes that covers most of Jewish history. Then you will want one on European history (with an emphasis on the Holocaust), one on Israel, and one on America. There are some excellent one-volume histories which read like an outline. Historical novels or histories written by novelists, like *The Jews* by Howard Fast, provide easy access.

5. Guides and Manuals

If you want to "do" Judaism and not just intellectualize about it, there are some excellent guides to the Jewish holidays (see *Sacred Celebrations* by Ron Isaacs and Kerry Olitzky) and how-to handbooks (like the one you are reading).

Things to remember:

1. Subscribe to Jewish newspapers and magazines. And don't forget to read about Israel.

2. Follow the weekly Torah portion. Keep a *Chumash* or a *Tehillim* (Book of Psalms) by your bed.

3. Keep up with the "Jewish" listings on the *New York Times* best seller list.

Key words and phrases:

Am ha'sefer עַם הַסֵּפֶר. People of the book.
Chumash חֻמָשׁ. From the word for "five"; the Torah (Five Books of Moses) arranged by weekly Torah and Haftarah portions.
Sefer סֵפֶר. Book, often referring to a sacred text.
Siddur סִדּוּר. Prayer book.

If you want to know more:

Barry Holtz, *The Schocken Guide to Jewish Books: Where to Start Reading About Jewish History, Literature, Culture, and Religion* (New York, 1992).

Choosing a Religious School
בֵּית סֵפֶר

The source:

"Teach them to your children" (Deuteronomy 11:19). "Train a child in the way to go, and even when old, he or she will not depart from it" (Proverbs 22:6). "The study of Torah is the most basic *mitzvah* of them all" (Babylonian Talmud, Shabbat 127a).

What you need to know:

1. A child's Jewish education should begin at a very early age.

2. Enroll your child in Jewish early-childhood, preschool, and primary programs.

3. Before choosing a school for your children, carefully consider the options in your area. Review the philosophy of education and goals of the school. Consider whether they are in harmony with your own.

4. Ask these questions and review the relevant documents:

   a. Does the school have a well-defined philosophy and mission statement (of purpose)?
   b. Does the school have a written curriculum that reflects its goals?
   c. Does the school have a pleasant atmosphere and a physical plant conducive to learning?
   d. Does the school have a trained educational director and experienced teaching staff?
   e. Does the school have strong community support?
   f. If needed, does the school provide opportunities for students with special learning needs?

Things to remember:

1. Always remember the importance of Jewish education in the home. Children should have opportunities early

in life to experience the sights, sounds, and flavors of Judaism in the home.

2. Raising Jewish children requires parents who lead Jewish lives. The home is the key, and Judaism must become a source of pleasure from the very beginning.

3. Many congregations provide innovative family-oriented educational programming that can assist in providing families with the knowledge and tools to bring Judaism back into their homes. Research the types of family programs that are available in your own area.

Key words and phrases:

Bet ha'sefer בֵּית הַסֵּפֶר (alternatively, *bet ha'midrash* בֵּית הַמִּדְרָשׁ). School.

Mishpachah מִשְׁפָּחָה. Family.

If you want to know more:

Hayim Halevy Donin, *To Raise a Jewish Child* (New York, 1977).

Ronald H. Isaacs, *Vesheenantam Levanekha: A Jewish Parents Handbook* (New York, 1995).

Kerry M. Olitzky et al., *When Your Jewish Child Asks Why: Answers to Tough Questions* (Hoboken, NJ, 1993).

How to Celebrate a *Simchah*
שִׂמְחָה

The source:

"You shall rejoice in your feast" (Deuteronomy 16:13).

What you need to know:

1. Jewish holidays and life-cycle events are cause for rejoicing and celebration. Such an event is called a *simchah,* the ultimate joyous event.

2. The celebration following a Jewish life-cycle event (like a Bar/Bat Mitzvah or a wedding) usually takes the form of a reception where food is served. This meal is called a *seudat mitzvah,* a "*mitzvah* meal." Often it is accompanied by singing and dancing.

3. Since a Jewish celebration is a sacred event, it should include activities of a religious nature. Here are some things that you might want to consider:

a. Serve kosher food so that all your guests, whether traditionally observant of the dietary laws or not, can enjoy the meal.
b. Begin the meal with the *Hamotzi* blessing over the bread, and conclude it with the reciting of the *Birkat Hamazon* (blessing after the meal).
c. Select spirited Jewish and Israeli music for group dancing and rejoicing.
d. Arrange in advance to give the leftover food to a local food bank.
e. Give any flowers to a local nursing home or hospital after the *simchah* has concluded.
f. In addition to giving friends of the Bar/Bat Mitzvah a souvenir "favor," plant a tree in Israel in their honor and give each a tree certificate as a memento. A Jewish book like this one is also a nice souvenir gift.
g. Ask guests to bring canned food, clothing, or toys to the party for subsequent distribution to the homeless.

h. Give a percentage of the cost of your *simchah* to a Hunger Fund (for example, Mazon, A Jewish Response to Hunger, 2940 West Boulevard, Suite 7, Los Angeles, CA 90064).

Things to remember:

Be certain that your Jewish celebration emphasizes Jewish values. These include compassion, dignity, justice, learning, generosity, humility, and modesty. Plan your celebration around these values.

Key words and phrases:

Seudat mitzvah סְעוּדַת מִצְוָה. Religious meal following Jewish life-cycle event.

Simchah שִׂמְחָה. Joyous celebration, usually a family life-cycle event.

If you want to know more:

Jeffrey K. Salkin, *Putting God on the Guest List* (Woodstock, VT, 1992).

How to Welcome Friends and Neighbors into Your Home (Or: Rules for Jewish Etiquette)
הַכְנָסַת אוֹרְחִים

The source:

"Because you were a stranger in a strange land" (Leviticus 19:34 and Exodus 12:49).

What you need to know:

Hospitality is simple. Make it easy for people to feel welcome in your home. Whatever you have, whether it is a lot or a little, share it with others.

Things to remember:

1. Remember that your ancestors were strangers in Egypt and America.

2. Extend a welcome to newcomers in your synagogue and school. Don't wait for someone to say hello to you. Extend yourself to them. As Rabbi Andy Warmflash, formerly of Congregation B'nai Tikvah in North Brunswick, New Jersey, likes to say each Shabbat, "After we make *Kiddush,* go up to someone whom you don't know or you don't know well and wish them *Shabbat Shalom."*

3. Welcoming strangers includes helping the hungry and the homeless.

Key words and phrases:

Hachnasat orchim הַכְנָסַת אוֹרְחִים. Welcoming guests or visitors; hospitality

Kol dichfin yeitei ve-yeichol כָּל דִכְפִין יֵיתֵי וְיֵכֹל. "Let all who are hungry come and eat," the phrase which begins the Passover seder.

If you want to know more:

Encyclopaedia Judaica (Jerusalem, 1978), 8:1030–33.
Ronald Isaacs and Kerry Olitzky, *Doing Mitzvot: Mitzvah Projects for Bar/Bat Mitzvah* (Hoboken, NJ, 1994).
Charles Kroloff, *When Elijah Knocks* (West Orange, NJ, 1992).
Barbara Fortgang Summers, *Community Responsibility in the Jewish Tradition* (New York, 1978).

More particulars:

1. In the medieval period, Jewish families used to display flags on their homes that would let travelers know they were welcome as guests.

2. *Ushpizin* is an unusual form of hospitality in which we invite exalted ancestors like Moses to dwell with us in the *sukkah* each year. This tradition comes from the core Jewish mystical text, the *Zohar.*

How to Give *Tzedakah*
צְדָקָה

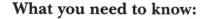

The source:

"Justice, charity, you shall pursue" (Deuteronomy 16:20).

What you need to know:

1. No matter whether you are rich or poor, you have an obligation to give *tzedakah*. It is our human way of helping God to establish balance in the order of the world.

2. Whatever you are doing, whatever holiday you are celebrating, whatever success you are acknowledging, re-member to share your joy—and express your gratitude to God—by giving *tzedakah*.

3. There are many ways to give from the heart. Money is only one of them.

Things to remember:

1. *Tzedakah* is a responsibility of all Jews, regardless of their socio-economic status. There is always someone less fortunate than you with whom you can share. One way we thank God for what we have is by sharing with others.

2. Establish your own pattern for giving, one that works for you and your family. Some people like to wait until they are finished paying bills at the end of the month. Others keep change in their pockets to be distributed while they are walking down the street. Still others keep *pushkes* at home, at work, everywhere—to remind them-selves and others. There are those who make "year-end" gifts to fit into the American tax year, and there are those who participate in "planned giving" programs which will ensure that their resources are available for *tzedakah* after they die. In our families, we like to empty the change in our pockets into a *tzedakah* box as we prepare for Shabbat, just before we light the candles and sit down for Shabbat dinner.

3. Every Jewish holiday has a *tzedakah* component. For example, one should set aside *maot chittin* (literally "wheat money") during Pesach so that the poor will be able to buy matzah. Remember: as you celebrate, share.

Key words and phrases:

Gemilut chasadim גְּמִילוּת חֲסָדִים. Loving acts of kindness, the giving of self to others.

Pushke (Yiddish) פּוּשְׁקֶע. *Tzedakah* container; for example, the JNF (Jewish National Fund) Blue Box.

Tzedakah צְדָקָה. Often translated as "charity"; we prefer "righteous giving."

If you want to know more:

Joel Lurie Grishaver and Beth Huppin, *Tzedakah, Gemilut Chasadim, and Ahavah: A Manual for World Repair* (Denver, 1983).

Danny Siegel, *Mitzvahs* (Pittsboro, NC, 1990).

More particulars:

Check out Maimonides' ladder of *tzedakah* in *The First How-To Handbook for Jewish Living.*

How to Arrange for a *Brit Milah* (Circumcision)
בְּרִית מִילָה

The source:

"Every male among you shall be circumcised. You shall circumcise the flesh of your foreskin, and that shall be the sign of the covenant between you and Me. At the age of eight days you shall be circumcised" (Genesis 17:10–12).

What you need to know:

1. Traditionally, it is the primary obligation of every Jewish father to circumcise his son. Since few parents have the competence to do this, it has become customary to appoint a *mohel* (ritual circumciser) to do this for them. If it is impossible to locate a *mohel,* a knowledgeable Jewish physician can be used.

2. The *Brit Milah* (circumcision ceremony) is always held on the eighth day after birth, even if it is the Sabbath or a Jewish holiday. (Some Reform rabbis permit the circumcision to take place on another day, under certain circumstances.)

3. Since the *Brit Milah* is a way of initiating a Jewish child into the House of Israel, it is appropriate to notify the entire community. In some communities young children of four or five visit the infant the night before and recite *Kriat Shema* at the baby's crib.

4. In addition to the *mohel,* the following take part in the ceremony:

> a. *Kvater.* The godfather; he brings the baby into the room where the circumcision will be performed.
> b. *Kvaterin.* The godmother; she accompanies the *kvater* in bringing the baby into the room.
> c. *Sandek.* He holds the baby while the circumcision is performed.

5. The Chair of Elijah, named in honor of Elijah the Prophet, is the chair or pillow on which the baby rests during the circumcision ceremony.

6. A festive meal follows the *Brit Milah.*

Things to remember:

1. There is a custom to place two candles in the room where the circumcision ceremony is to take place, as a symbol of God's Light and Presence.

2. Before the ceremony begins, some parents follow the beautiful custom of saying a few words about the meaning and choice of the baby's name.

3. The ceremony begins when the godparents bring the baby into the room where the *Brit Milah* will be performed.

4. The *sandek* holds the baby and the officiant then says this blessing:

בָּרוּךְ אַתָּה יהוה אֱלֹהֵינוּ מֶלֶךְ הָעוֹלָם, אֲשֶׁר קִדְּשָׁנוּ בְּמִצְוֹתָיו וְצִוָּנוּ עַל הַמִּילָה:

Baruch atah Adonai elohaynu melech ha'olam asher kidshanu b'mitzvotav ve'tzivanu al ha'milah.

Praise are You, Adonai our God, Sovereign of the Universe, who made us holy through *mitzvot* and instructed us concerning circumcision.

5. After the circumcision has been performed, the father, and quite often the mother too, recites this blessing:

בָּרוּךְ אַתָּה יהוה אֱלֹהֵינוּ מֶלֶךְ הָעוֹלָם, אֲשֶׁר קִדְּשָׁנוּ בְּמִצְוֹתָיו וְצִוָּנוּ לְהַכְנִיסוֹ בִּבְרִיתוֹ שֶׁל אַבְרָהָם אָבִינוּ:

Baruch atah Adonai elohaynu melech ha'olam asher kidshanu b'mitzvotav ve'tzivanu le'hachniso be'vrito shel Avraham Avinu.

Praised are You, Adonai our God, Sovereign of the Universe, who made us holy through *mitzvot* and instructed us to bring our son into the covenant of Abraham our ancestor.

6. All of those present then respond:

כְּשֵׁם שֶׁנִּכְנַס לַבְּרִית, כֵּן יִכָּנֵס לְתוֹרָה וּלְחֻפָּה וּלְמַעֲשִׂים טוֹבִים:

Keshem she'nichnas labrit ken yikanes le'torah ule'chuppah ule'ma'asim tovim.

As he has entered the covenant, so too may he enter a life of Torah, marriage, and good deeds.

7. The officiant then recites a blessing over a cup of wine and formally gives the baby his Hebrew name.

Key words and phrases:

Brit Milah בְּרִית מִילָה. Circumcision.
Hatafat dam brit הַטָּפַת דַּם בְּרִית. Symbolic circumcision letting out a drop of blood.
Kvater קוואַטער. Godfather.
Kvaterin קוואַטערין. Godmother.
Mohel מוֹהֵל (Mohelet מוֹהֶלֶת). Ritual circumciser.
Sandek סַנְדָק. One who holds the child during circumcision.
Shalom zachar שָׁלוֹם זָכָר. Ceremony for welcoming the son.

If you want to know more:

Lewis M. Barth, ed., *Berit Mila in the Reform Context* (New York, 1990).
Ronald H. Isaacs, *Rites of Passage: Guide to the Jewish Life Cycle* (Hoboken, NJ, 1992).

More particulars:

1. Mornings are preferable to afternoons for a circumcision ceremony, so as to show zeal in the performance of this *mitzvah*.

2. Some families hold a *Shalom Zachar,* a sort of welcome ceremony for the new son, on the Friday evening prior to the *Brit Milah,* either in the synagogue or at home. As friends and neighbors gather, the rabbi or the parent speaks words of Torah in honor of the occasion and blesses the child.

3. If a baby cannot be circumcised on the eighth day for reasons of health, the *Brit Milah* may be postponed.

4. If a baby is medically circumcised but the proper blessings are not recited, and the ceremony did not take place on the eighth day, then a symbolic circumcision, called a *hatafat dam brit,* is performed. This ceremony involves a pinprick that lets out a spot of blood on the genital. It must be done either by a *mohel* or a qualified Jewish physician. The symbolic circumcision is also used in the conversion to Judaism of a non-Jewish male child or adult who has been surgically circumcised.

How to Arrange for a
Simchat Bat
(Female Hebrew Naming and
Covenant Ceremony)
שִׂמְחַת בַּת

The source:

The custom of naming children after other persons began in approximately the sixth century B.C.E.

What you need to know:

1. Traditionally, a Jewish girl is named in the synagogue, usually on a day when the Torah is read. However, home ceremonies are also nice.

2. Although there is no prescribed time for naming a Jewish girl, we recommend that you do so as soon as possible after birth.

3. You may want to include these elements if you design your own naming ceremony:

a. The baby is carried into the room. Candles are lit. (*Note:* if the ceremony takes place on the Sabbath or a Jewish festival, the candles should be lit at the proper candle-lighting time.) Recently, a blessing to be recited after the lighting of the candles has been suggested:

בָּרוּךְ אַתָּה יהוה אֱלֹהֵינוּ מֶלֶךְ הָעוֹלָם, אֲשֶׁר קִדְּשָׁנוּ בְּמִצְוֹתָיו
וְצִוָּנוּ עַל קִדּוּשׁ הַחַיִּים:

Baruch atah Adonai elohaynu melech ha'olam asher kid-shanu b'mitzvotav vitzivanu al kiddush ha'chayim.

Praised are You, Adonai our God, Sovereign of the Universe, who made us holy through *mitzvot* and instructed us to sanctify life.

b. Next, chant this blessing over a cup of wine:

בָּרוּךְ אַתָּה יהוה אֱלֹהֵינוּ מֶלֶךְ הָעוֹלָם, בּוֹרֵא פְּרִי הַגָּפֶן:

Baruch atah Adonai elohaynu melech ha'olam boray pri ha'gafen.

Praised are You, Adonai our God, Sovereign of the Universe, who creates the fruit of the vine.

c. Next, recite this conventional paragraph of the ceremony:

בָּרוּךְ אַתָּה יהוה אֱלֹהֵינוּ מֶלֶךְ הָעוֹלָם, אֲשֶׁר קִדֵּשׁ יָדִיד מִבֶּטֶן, אֵל חַי חֶלְקֵנוּ צוּרֵנוּ, צַוֵּה לְהַצִּיל יְדִידוּת שְׁאֵרֵנוּ מִשַּׁחַת, לְמַעַן בְּרִיתוֹ. בָּרוּךְ אַתָּה יְיָ, כּוֹרֵת הַבְּרִית:
אֱלוֹהַּ כָּל הַבְּרִיאוֹת קַיֵּם אֶת־הַיַּלְדָּה הַזֹּאת לְאָבִיהָ וּלְאִמָּהּ:

You have sanctified Your beloved from the womb and established Your holy covenant throughout the generations. May devotion to the covenant continue to sustain us as a people. Praised are You, God, who has established the covenant.

d. Ask the participants to respond:

כְּשֵׁם שֶׁנִּכְנֶסֶת לַבְּרִית, כֵּן תִּכָּנְסִי לְתוֹרָה וּלְחֻפָּה וּלְמַעֲשִׂים טוֹבִים:

K'shem shenichneset la'brit ken tikansi l'torah ul'chuppah ule'ma'asim tovim.

As she has entered the covenant, so may she enter a life devoted to Torah, the marriage canopy, and the accomplishment of good deeds.

e. This is followed by the actual naming, in Hebrew, of the baby girl.

f. Conclude the ceremony by having the parents recite the prayer for the gift of life, called the *Shehecheyanu:*

בָּרוּךְ אַתָּה יהוה אֱלֹהֵינוּ מֶלֶךְ הָעוֹלָם, שֶׁהֶחֱיָנוּ וְקִיְּמָנוּ וְהִגִּיעָנוּ, לַזְּמַן הַזֶּה:

Baruch atah Adonai elohenyu melech ha'olam she-hecheyanu ve'keemanu ve'heegeeyanu lazman ha'zeh.

59

Praised are You, Adonai our God, Sovereign of the ZUniverse, who has kept us alive and sustained us and enabled us to reach this happy day.

g. A festive meal follows, where the blessing over the bread (*Hamotzi*) and the blessing after the meal (*Birkat Hamazon*) are appropriate.

Key words and phrases:

Brit ha'chayim בְּרִית חַיִּים. Literally "covenant of life"; often refers to naming ceremony for Jewish girls.

Simchat bat שִׂמְחַת בַּת. Literally "joy of the daughter"; another designation of the naming ceremony for girls.

Zeved ha'bat זֶבֶד הַבַּת. Literally "celebration for the gift of a daughter"; Sephardic naming ceremony for girls.

If you want to know more:

Ronald H. Isaacs, *Rites of Passage: Guide to the Jewish Life Cycle* (Hoboken, NJ, 1992).

How to Arrange for a *Pidyon Haben* (Redemption of Firstborn Son)
פִּדְיוֹן הַבֵּן

The source:

"From a month old a child shall be redeemed" (Numbers 18:16).

What you need to know:

1. A *Pidyon Haben* ceremony (i.e., redemption of the firstborn son) takes place thirty days after birth.

2. If the thirty-first day falls on a Sabbath or festival, the redemption ceremony is postponed to the following day.

3. The *Pidyon Haben* ceremony generally takes place in one's home during the daytime.

4. In order to conduct the *Pidyon Haben* ceremony, you need a cup of wine, a *challah* (part of the festive meal), a *Kohen* (priestly descendant), the firstborn male child and his parents, five shekels (silver dollars are often used today, or you can purchase silver coins specially minted for the *Pidyon Haben* ceremony which are often donated to charity afterwards), and the officiant, usually a rabbi or cantor, who helps to facilitate the conducting of the ceremony.

Things to remember:

Please note: Since the Reform movement has removed the class distinctions of *Kohen, Levi,* and Israelite, most Reform rabbis (including one of the authors) do not encourage this ceremony as detailed below. Instead, one should encourage the child who is the focus of the ceremony to serve God in a variety of ways.

1. The following is a sample *Pidyon Haben* ceremony which you may use or adapt in any way you see fit:

a. The father hands his son to the *kohen* and says the following:

זֶה בְּנִי בְכוֹרִי וְהוּא פֶּטֶר רֶחֶם לְאִמּוֹ, וְהַקָּדוֹשׁ בָּרוּךְ הוּא צִוָּה לִפְדּוֹתוֹ, שֶׁנֶּאֱמַר, וּפְדוּיָו מִבֶּן חֹדֶשׁ תִּפְדֶּה בְּעֶרְכְּךָ כֶּסֶף חֲמֵשֶׁת שְׁקָלִים בְּשֶׁקֶל הַקּוֹדֶשׁ עֶשְׂרִים גֵּרָה הוּא. וְנֶאֱמַר, קַדֶּשׁ לִי כָל בְּכוֹר פֶּטֶר כָּל רֶחֶם בִּבְנֵי יִשְׂרָאֵל בָּאָדָם וּבַבְּהֵמָה, לִי הוּא:

This my firstborn is the firstborn of his mother, and God has directed us to redeem him, as it is written in the Torah: "when he is one month old you shall redeem him for five shekels." And it is written: "Sanctify unto Me every firstborn Israelite; he is Mine."

b. Next the father places the five silver shekels before the *kohen* and the *kohen* asks:

מַה בָּעֵית טְפֵי לִיתֵּן לִי בִּנְךָ בְכוֹרָךְ שֶׁהוּא פֶּטֶר רֶחֶם לְאִמּוֹ, אוֹ בָּעֵית לִפְדּוֹתוֹ בְּעַד חָמֵשׁ סְלָעִים כִּדְמְחַיַּבְתָּ מִדְּאוֹרַיְתָא:

What is your preference—to give me your firstborn son or to redeem him for five shekels, as you are commanded to do in the Torah?

c. The father gives the five shekels to the *kohen* and says:

חָפֵץ אֲנִי לִפְדּוֹת אֶת בְּנִי וְהֵילָךְ דְּמֵי פִדְיוֹנוֹ כִּדְמְחַיַּבְתִּי מִדְּאוֹרַיְתָא:

I want to redeem my son. Here is the equivalent of five shekels, and thus I fulfill my obligation according to the Torah.

d. The *kohen* accepts the redemption money and returns the child to the father, whereupon the father recites:

בָּרוּךְ אַתָּה יהוה אֱלֹהֵינוּ מֶלֶךְ הָעוֹלָם, אֲשֶׁר קִדְּשָׁנוּ בְּמִצְוֹתָיו וְצִוָּנוּ עַל פִּדְיוֹן הַבֵּן:

Baruch atah Adonai elohaynu melech ha'olam asher kidshanu b'mitzvotav ve'tzivanu al pidyon ha'ben.

Praised are You, Adonai our God, Sovereign of the Universe, who made us holy with your *mitzvot* and instructed us concerning the redemption of the first-born.

e. Father and mother together say the prayer for the gift of life:

בָּרוּךְ אַתָּה יהוה אֱלֹהֵינוּ מֶלֶךְ הָעוֹלָם, שֶׁהֶחֱיָנוּ וְקִיְּמָנוּ וְהִגִּיעָנוּ, לַזְּמַן הַזֶּה:

Baruch atah Adonai elohaynu melech ha'olam she-hecheyanu ve'keemanu ve'heegeeyanu lazman ha'zeh.

Praised are You, Adonai our God, Sovereign of the Universe, who has kept us alive, sustained us, and enabled us to reach this day.

e. The *kohen* then holds the coins and says:

זֶה תַּחַת זֶה זֶה חִלּוּף זֶה זֶה מָחוּל עַל זֶה. וְיִכָּנֵס זֶה הַבֵּן לַחַיִּים, לְתוֹרָה וּלְחֻפָּה וּלְמַעֲשִׂים טוֹבִים, אָמֵן:

I accept the five shekels and hereby declare your son redeemed. May he be granted a complete and full life, live in devotion to the Torah and with reverence for God. As this child has attained redemption, so may it be God's will that he attain the blessings of Torah, marriage, and a life of good deeds.

f. The *kohen* blesses the child with the threefold priestly blessing.

יְשִׂמְךָ אֱלֹהִים כְּאֶפְרַיִם וְכִמְנַשֶּׁה.

Yiseemcha Eloheem k'efrayim v'cheem'nasheh.

May God make you like Ephraim and Manasseh.

יְבָרֶכְךָ יהוה וְיִשְׁמְרֶךָ.

Yevarechecha Adonai v'yishmerecha.

May God bless and keep you.

יָאֵר יהוה פָּנָיו אֵלֶיךָ וִיחֻנֶּךָּ.

Ya'er Adonai panav eylecha veechuneka.

May God's Presence shine on and be good to you.

יִשָּׂא יהוה פָּנָיו אֵלֶיךָ וְיָשֵׂם לְךָ שָׁלוֹם.

Yisa Adonai panav eylecha ve'yasem lecha shalom.

May God's face turn toward you and give you peace.

2. A festive meal concludes the ceremony. It ought to begin with the recitation of the blessing over the bread (*Hamotzi*) before the meal, and should conclude with the blessing after the meal (*Birkat Hamazon*) following it.

Key words and phrases:

Kohen כֹּהֵן. Descendant of the priestly caste.
Pidyon Haben פִּדְיוֹן הַבֵּן. Redemption of the firstborn son.

If you want to know more:

Ronald H. Isaacs, *Rites of Passage: Guide to the Jewish Life Cycle* (Hoboken, NJ, 1992).
Leo Trepp, *The Complete Book of Jewish Observance* (New York, 1980).

More particulars:

1. Traditional Jewish law requires that a *Pidyon Haben* be performed if the child is male and the first "issue" of the mother's womb. If the child's father is a *kohen* or levite, he automatically belongs to the special caste of ministers called *kohanim* and *levi'im* and need not have a *Pidyon Haben*. Also, if the mother of the child is the daughter of a *kohen* or *levi* the rite is not performed.

2. A male child born by Caesarean operation does not have to be redeemed because Jewish law does not consider such a child to have "issued forth" from the womb.

3. A son born of a woman who previously had a miscarriage does not require a *Pidyon Haben,* nor does a son born to a woman who previously had a stillbirth.

4. If a man marries twice, the firstborn son of each wife must be redeemed.

5. In recent years some families have created a personalized ritual for their firstborn daughters. Such ceremonies are known by different names, including *pidyon habat*

(redemption of the firstborn daughter) and *kiddush petter rechem* (sanctification of the one who opens the womb). These ceremonies often include a dialogue between the officiant and the parents related to the importance of consecrating firstborn children, as well as an exchange of coins, which are often donated to charity in honor of the firstborn daughter. Such ceremonies offer an alternative to those uncomfortable with social-class distinctions.

Family Blessings
בִּרְכוֹת הַמִּשְׁפָּחָה

The source:

The first source for the family blessings is Genesis 48:20. In this passage, Jacob blesses his grandchildren Ephraim and Menasseh. The second source for the family blessings is the Book of Numbers 6:23–26. In this section God speaks to Moses who in turn is told to speak to his brother Aaron. God then presents Aaron with the blessing, which has come to be known as the three-fold priestly blessing.

What you need to know:

1. It is customary for parents to bless their children before sitting down to a Sabbath meal. The blessing provides parents with a privileged opportunity to express appreciation for their children.

2. Through the touch of a parent's hands or the sound of a parent's voice, children can feel and respond to the love and affection their family has for them.

3. The blessing for boys invokes the shining examples of Jacob's grandchildren Ephraim and Manasseh, who, although raised in Egypt, did not lose their identity as Jews.

4. The blessing for girls refers to the four matriarchs, Sarah, Rebekah, Rachel and Leah, all of whom were known for their concern and compassion for others.

5. The family blessings conclude with the priestly benediction invoking God's protection and peace.

6. For boys, parents gently place both hands on his head and recite:

יְשִׂמְךָ אֱלֹהִם כְּאֶפְרַיִם וְכִמְנַשֶּׁה.

Yiseemcha Eloheem k'Efraim v'cheemenasseh

66

May God make you like Ephraim and Menasseh.
(Genesis 48:20)

For girls, parents approach each daughter and gently place both their hands upon her head and recite:

יְשִׂימֵךְ אֱלֹהִים כְּשָׂרָה, רִבְקָה, רָחֵל, וְלֵאָה,

Yesimech Eloheem k'Sarah, Rivka, Rachel v'Leah

May God make you like Sarah, Rebekah, Rachel and Leah.

For both boys and girls, conclude with the priestly blessing.

יְבָרֶכְךָ יְיָ וְיִשְׁמְרֶךָ,

Yevarechecha Adonai v'yishmerecha

May God bless and keep you.

יָאֵר יְיָ פָּנָיו אֵלֶיךָ וִיחֻנֶּךָּ,

Ya'er Adonai panav eylecha veechuneka

May God's Presence shine and be good to you.

יִשָּׂא יְיָ פָּנָיו אֵלֶיךָ וְיָשֵׂם לְךָ שָׁלוֹם.

Yisa Adonai panav eylecha veyasem lecha shalom.

May God's face turn toward you and give you peace.

Key words and phrases:

Birkat hacohanim בִּרְכַּת הַכֹּהֲנִים Priestly blessing.

If you want to know more:

Ronald H. Isaacs and Kerry M. Olizky, *Sacred Celebrations: A Jewish Holiday Handbook* (Hoboken, 1994).

Preparing for Shabbat
הֲכָנָה לְשַׁבָּת

The source:

"You shall labor for six days and do all your work, but the seventh day is a Sabbath of Adonai your God: You shall not do any work" (Exodus 20:9–10).

What you need to know:

1. In the Jewish mystical tradition, the Sabbath has been portrayed as a bride or queen who visits homes every week of the year. Jewish people are expected to get ready—physically and spiritually—to greet this special guest.

2. Polish the Shabbat candlesticks and *Kiddush* wine cup a few days before the Sabbath begins.

3. Clean your house before the Sabbath actually begins and prepare your Shabbat dinner. Make sure you have the following items: two *challot* to represent the double portion of manna in the desert, saving one for Shabbat lunch, kosher wine, a pretty tablecloth, and a table set with your best dinnerware. Decorating the table with fresh flowers will help to create a *Shabbesdik* ("Shabbat-like") atmosphere. Naturally the meal you serve should be a special one.

4. It is customary to wash oneself and put on fresh clothing for Shabbat, symbolizing readiness to welcome the Sabbath into one's home.

5. To add to the mood of caring and sharing, many families make it a habit to drop some coins in a *pushke* (*tzedakah* box), before lighting the Sabbath candles. When the *tzedakah* box is full, decide as a family to which organization you want to donate the money.

Things to remember:

1. It is a nice gesture to invite friends to your home for the Sabbath meal in keeping with the important Jewish value of *hachnasat orchim* (hospitality).

2. Since singing songs is an important tradition during the Sabbath meal, you may want to obtain (or even prepare yourself) a small booklet with the Shabbat songs that you sing from week to week. Be sure to have enough copies so that everyone can participate. Use English and Hebrew songs, and be creative!

3. Family cooperation is indispensable to the completion of all pre-Shabbat tasks. Give each member of the family something to do so that everyone can help get ready for Shabbat.

4. According to Jewish tradition, we get an extra soul during Shabbat.

5. Invite the angels to accompany you during Shabbat. (That's what *Shalom Aleichem* is all about.)

Key words and phrases:

Hachanah le'shabbat הֲכָנָה לְשַׁבָּת. Preparation for the Sabbath.
Pushke (Yiddish) פּוּשְׁקֶע. *Tzedakah* (charity) box.
Zemirot זְמִירוֹת. Sabbath table songs.

If you want to know more:

Ronald H. Isaacs, *Shabbat Delight: A Celebration in Stories, Games and Songs* (Hoboken, NJ, 1987).
—— and Kerry M. Olitzky, *Sacred Celebrations: A Jewish Holiday Handbook* (Hoboken, NJ, 1994).

Getting Ready for Rosh Hashanah
הֲכָנָה לְרֹאשׁ הַשָּׁנָה

The source:

"In the seventh month, on the first day of the month, shall be a solemn rest for you, a memorial proclaimed with the blast of horns, a holy convocation" (Leviticus: 23:24).

What you need to know:

1. The month of Elul, which immediately precedes Rosh Hashanah (and the month of Tishri), is spent in introspection, what the tradition calls *cheshbon hanefesh*. Thus, the best way to get ready for Rosh Hashanah is by looking deeply into yourself, trying to assess where you have gone so that you can determine where you want to go. This is happy time but a serious soul-searching business, as well.

2. Depending on the tradition of the community, penitential prayers called *Selichot* are said during the month of Elul. These prayers culminate in a *Selichot* service, generally held at midnight on Saturday just prior to Rosh Hashanah. (In some years, the service is held the preceding Saturday night.)

Things to remember:

1. While Rosh Hashanah has become a High Holiday in the modern Jewish community, it is really less significant than Shabbat. It begins the important Ten Days of Awe which culminate in Yom Kippur. Thus, a lot of the rules for Shabbat, but not all of them, also apply on Rosh Hashanah. The major thing to remember is to make sure that what you do is in the spirit of the holiday.

2. Use a round *challah* for Rosh Hashanah to represent the cycle of life, instead of the braided one reserved for Shabbat.

3. Prepare your table (eat in the dining room, not the kitchen) with flowers and your best dinnerware. Remember to invite guests, especially those new to the community who do not have local family to share the holiday together.

4. If you wear a *kittel* (white robe-like garment) during the holidays, make sure you know where it is.

5. Send out holiday cards in advance. Make your holiday calls, especially to those you haven't spoken to in a long time. Use the preholiday period as a time to mend broken bridges with estranged friends and family.

Key words and phrases:

Leshanah tovah tikateivu לְשָׁנָה טוֹבָה תִּכָּתֵבוּ. "May you be inscribed [in the book of life] for the new year"; traditional greeting for Rosh Hashanah.

Rosh Hashanah רֹאשׁ הַשָּׁנָה. Literally, "head of the year"; new year.

Shofar שׁוֹפָר. Ram's horn used on Rosh Hashanah (and a few other occasions) to call us to the work of *teshuvah* (repentance).

Yom Hazikaron יוֹם הַזִּכָּרוֹן. Day of Remembrance, alternative name for Rosh Hashanah.

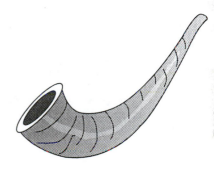

If you want to know more:

Ronald H. Isaacs and Kerry Olitzky, *Sacred Celebrations: A Jewish Holiday Handbook* (Hoboken, NJ, 1994).

More particulars:

Prepare apples and honey to usher in the sweet year. Hint: sprinkle a little lemon juice on your sliced apples to prevent them from turning brown. After you say *Hamotzi*, say the following (then dip your apples in honey and enjoy!):

יְהִי רָצוֹן מִלְפָנֶיךָ יהוה אֱלֹהֵינוּ וֵאלֹהֵי אֲבוֹתֵינוּ שֶׁתְּחַדֵּשׁ עָלֵינוּ שָׁנָה טוֹבָה וּמְתוּקָה.

Yehi ratzon milfanecha Adonai elohaynu vaylohay avotenu shetechadesh alaynu shanah tovah u'metukah.

71

May it be Your will, Adonai our God, that Your renew for us a good and sweet year.

בָּרוּךְ אַתָּה יהוה אֱלֹהֵינוּ מֶלֶךְ הָעוֹלָם, בּוֹרֵא פְּרִי הָעֵץ:

Baruch atah Adonai elohaynu melech ha'olam boray pri ha'etz.

Praised are You, Adonai our God, Sovereign of the Universe, who creates the fruit of the tree.

How to Construct Your Own Theology
תּוֹרַת הַדָּת

The source:

"I am Adonai your God, who brought you out of the land of Egypt, out of the house of bondage" (Exodus 20:1).

What you need to know:

1. While the notion of theology in Judaism is a relatively new phenomenon, don't leave the construction of your theology to theologians. While you should consult the thoughts of others in order to determine whether you agree or disagree, your beliefs are more truly expressed by what you do than by what you say. So don't just say what you believe, express your beliefs in action.

2. To make a statement of your personal theology, begin with the words "I believe . . ." and fill in whatever should come next. That's all you need to get started. Encourage others to do the same. Do not criticize the beliefs of others. You will share many common beliefs with others, but you will disagree as well—even with people with whom you study, pray, and play.

Things to remember:

1. Before you venture out on your own and try constructing your own theology, consult those who have come before you. Consider also the works of contemporary theologians like Eliezer Berkovits, Eugene Borowitz, Emil Fackenheim, Abraham Joshua Heschel, and Mordecai Kaplan. Read and study. Remember, there is more out there than just what appears on the *New York Times* bestseller list. The study of a sacred text—and its implicit theology—will help you form your own.

2. Don't be afraid to reconsider your beliefs, to change your opinions, as you open yourself up to new experiences of Jewish living.

3. Struggle for consistency in your belief system, however difficult it may be to achieve, but don't be so inflexible that you cannot live with contradictions.

4. Think with your heart and your mind.

5. A belief in God is central to Jewish theology.

6. Test out your beliefs in the context of the world in which you live.

If you want to know more:

Eugene B. Borowitz, *Choices in Modern Jewish Thought* (New York, 1983).

Arthur Green, *Seek My Face, Speak My Name: A Contemporary Jewish Theology* (Northvale, NJ, 1992).

Ron Isaacs, *Close Encounters with God* (Northvale, NJ, In Press).

Louis Jacobs, *A Jewish Theology* (New York, 1973).

Nathan Rotenstreich, *Jewish Philosophy in Modern Times* (New York, 1968).

Planning a Jewish Trip
טִיּוּל

The source:

"Jews are an omniterritorial people. They are everywhere. There is never a first Jew in any place. There was always a Jew there before" (Jacob Rader Marcus, historian).

What you need to know:

Bring a pair of portable candlesticks, *siddur,* and anything else you need for personal observance while traveling.

Things to remember:

1. Chabad-Lubavitch is everywhere. While you may not share the Chabad-Lubavitch approach to Judaism, know that you have a friend representing the Jewish community in most places wherever you travel in the world.

2. Many of the larger cities in United States and Canada have prepared books called "A Jewish Guide to _____." When planning a trip, contact the local Jewish Federation or Jewish Community Center at your destination.

3. Before you set out on a journey, don't forget to recite the traveler's prayer (*tefillat ha'derech*), available in most prayer books and in our *First How-To Handbook for Jewish Living*. Small laminated wallet-sized copies of *tefillat ha'derech* are available in most Jewish book stores.

4. Depending on your dietary requirements, check out what may be available ahead of time, then plan accordingly. Some people always travel with a kosher salami in their suitcase, just in case.

Key words and phrases:

Tiyul טִיּוּל. A trip, usually in Israel.

If you want to know more:

Warren Freedman, *The Selective Guide for the Jewish Traveler* (New York, 1972).

Stephen Massil, *The Jewish Travel Guide* (London, published annually).

Bernard Postal and Samuel Abramson, *The Landmarks of a People: A Guide to Jewish Sites in Europe* (New York, 1971).

Bernard Postal and Lionel Kopman, *A Jewish Tourist's Guide to the U.S.* (Philadelphia, 1954).

Richard Siegel, Sharon Strassfeld, and Michael Strassfeld, *The Jewish Catalogue* (Philadelphia, 1973, 1976). See "The Jewish Yellow Pages."

Alan M. Tigay, *The Jewish Traveler* (Northvale, NJ, 1994).

More particulars:

The national or international body of each of the various religious movements generally has a guide to affiliated institutions around the world. Contact these organizations for help in locating synagogues (and other Jewish community resources), especially to find a daily *minyan* and Shabbat services:

Agudath Israel
84 William Street
New York, NY 10038

Chabad-Lubavitch
770 Eastern Parkway
Brooklyn, NY 11213

Federation of Reconstructionist Synagogues and Havurot
15 West 86th Street
New York, NY 10024

Union of American Hebrew Congregations
838 Fifth Avenue
New York, NY 10021

Union of Orthodox Jewish Congregations of America
333 Seventh Avenue
New York, NY 10001

Union of Sephardic Congregations
8 West 70th Street
New York, New York 10023

United Synagogue of Conservative Judaism
115 Fifth Avenue
New York, NY 10010

World Union for Progressive Judaism
838 Fifth Avenue
New York, NY 10021

How to Bury Ritual Objects or Place Them in a *Genizah*
גְּנִיזָה

The source:

Various sources, including Megillah 26b; Hilchot Yesodei Hatorah 6:8.

What you need to know:

While there is no specific ritual for burying ritual objects, people often recite poetic texts about study and the sacredness of Torah in preparation for burying a ritual object or ceremoniously placing something in a *genizah*.

Things to remember:

Sacred objects (like Torah scrolls and *tefillin*) and sacred writings (Bibles, prayer books) should be treated with respect. That's why we don't simply throw them away when they are no longer suitable for use.

Key words and phrases:

Genizah גְּנִיזָה. From the word for "hidden"; usually a closet, room, or hidden place in a synagogue where old prayer books and other sacred books are kept prior to burial.
Sefarim genuzim סְפָרִים גְּנֻזִים. Books to be hidden away.

If you want to know more:

Moses Maimonides, *Mishneh Torah,* Hilchot Yesodei Hatorah.

More particulars:

1. Some things may not require special treatment according to Jewish law yet Jewish sensitivities require that they be handled specially. For example, you may want to

consider using the *lulav* for Sukkot for lighting the fire to burn your *chametz* prior to Pesach. And use your *etrog* for jam (see "Making *Etrog* Jam").

2. While we must be careful about using God's name in vain, it seems to us that photocopy paper with God's name on it should be recycled for further use rather than buried. This is not in accordance with traditional practice, but it seems to us that it makes sense in the contemporary context. While some Orthodox Jews may question this approach, many members of the Reform, Reconstructionist, and Conservative movements will find it appropriate.

3. There is an ancient custom of honoring a dead person by burying sacred books (or Torah scrolls) next to the coffin.

Making a *Shivah* Call
שִׁבְעָה

The source:

"May the Almighty comfort you among the mourners for Zion and Jerusalem" (traditional greeting of comfort to mourners).

What you need to know:

1. If you join the bereaved right after the interment, you should arrange their first meal (called the *seudah ha'havra'ah,* "meal of consolation"). Don't expect to be entertained or served.

2. When you approach the home of the bereaved, especially right after the funeral, there may be a pitcher of water next to the door. If you are comfortable in doing so, wash your hands prior to entering the home. This reflects the ancient custom of ridding oneself of the impurities associated with death. Upon doing so, it is customary to recite these words:

> You will swallow up death forever;
> And Adonai, God will wipe away tears from off all faces; And the reproach of Your people will You take away from off all the earth;
> For Adonai has said it.
>
> Isaiah 25:8

3. When you enter a *shivah* home, remember that it is a house in which people are mourning. Participate in prayer if you visit during the time in which prayers are being said. Try to comfort the bereaved person by speaking from the heart. Avoid truisms and cliches. And don't feel obliged to fill up the silence. Often, your presence alone is comforting. Indeed, Rabbi Yochanan taught, "Comforters are not permitted to say a word until the mourner begins the conversation" (Babylonian Talmud, Moed Katan 28b).

Things to remember:

1. The term *shivah* is taken from the word for "seven," referring to the seven days of intensive mourning following the death of a loved one. The name *shivah* is generally applied to everything related to mourning during this period. Thus, we speak of the *shivah* house, the *shivah minyan,* and making a *shivah* call.

2. It is customary for a mourner concluding *shivah* to take a walk around the block, "to get up from *shivah,*" as a way of symbolically reentering routine life. If you happen to make your call at the end of the *shivah* period, be prepared to take this walk with your bereaved friend or relative.

3. For a variety of reasons which primarily have to do with focusing the attention of the mourners on the process of mourning rather than on themselves, it is customary to cover the mirrors in a *shivah* home. Do not uncover them.

Key words and phrases:

Avelut אֲבֵילוּת. Period of mourning following the interment.

Chesed shel emet חֶסֶד שֶׁל אֱמֶת. True piety, referring to honoring the dead and comforting mourners.

Sheloshim שְׁלוֹשִׁים. Twenty-three-day period of less intensive mourning which follows *shivah,* concluding on the thirtieth day after the funeral.

Shivah שִׁבְעָה. From the word for "seven"; the seven days of intensive mourning following a death.

If you want to know more:

Ronald H. Isaacs and Kerry M. Olitzky, *A Jewish Mourner's Handbook* (Hoboken, NJ, 1991).

Maurice Lamm, *The Jewish Way in Death and Mourning* (New York, 1969).

Sitting *Shivah* and Observing the *Sheloshim*
שִׁבְעָה וּשְׁלוֹשִׁים

The source:

The Bible records various instances of the seven-day mourning ritual (*shivah*). For example, in Genesis 50:10 Jacob dies and Joseph mourns for his father for a period of seven days (see also Amos 8:10).

What you need to know:

1. The traditional period of "sitting *shivah*" (as the seven-day mourning period is called) begins immediately after the funeral and concludes after the morning (*shacharit*) service six days later. (Among some Reform and Reconstructionist Jews, the period of mourning is less than seven days.)

2. The laws of mourning are suspended on the Sabbath that occurs during the *shivah* period, but despite this the Sabbath day counts as one of the seven days for *shivah*.

3. Jewish tradition encourages the ritual washing of hands before entering the house of *shivah* after the funeral as an act of spiritual cleansing.

4. A seven-day *shivah* candle is lit immediately when one returns to the house of *shivah* after the burial.

5. It is customary to cover all mirrors in a house of *shivah* since mourners should not be concerned with issues of vanity.

6. Traditionally, the mourner remains in the house of *shivah* during the entire week. Food is provided by friends, and prayer services are arranged and led by friends in the house of *shivah*.

6. As a sign of mourning, mourners traditionally refrain from wearing leather shoes (specifically, shoes with

leather soles) because they are considered a sign of luxury and vain comfort. In addition, the mourners sit on low stools or benches as a symbol of their lowly state. Traditional mourners do not watch television, study (except the books of Job, Lamentations, and Jeremiah and laws pertaining to mourning), wear new clothes, or make love with their spouses.

7. Mourners during the period of *shivah* may attend synagogue services on Friday evening and Saturday morning and afternoon. Otherwise, prayer should take place at home. When mourners arrive at the synagogue on Shabbat, they enter after *Lecha Dodi* is recited. As they do so, the congregants turn and say, "May God comfort you among the mourners of Zion and Jerusalem."

8. *Shivah* ends on the morning of the seventh day. It is customary for mourners to take a short walk with their family and close friends. The walk symbolizes the return to everyday life.

9. When visiting a house of *shivah* it is customary to bring food (cake, a fruit basket, and the like). Of course making a donation in memory of the deceased is a most appropriate way of paying tribute.

10. During the period of *sheloshim* (the twenty-three days after *shivah* ends) mourners are permitted to return to work and their regular routine. They recite the Mourner's *Kaddish* each day, however (and continue to do so for eleven months), and moderate their leisure-time activities.

Things to remember:

1. During *shivah*, friends and family will often feel uncomfortable and not be exactly sure what to say to the mourner. Searching for words to give the mourner comfort, they may feel inclined not to speak until the mourner speaks to them. In fact, this is the advice that Jewish tradition offers the individual making a *shivah* call.

2. If the holiday of Rosh Hashanah, Yom Kippur, Passover, Shavuot, or Sukkot occurs during the *shivah* period, the *shivah* ends when the holiday begins even if it is not yet

the seventh day. If the interment takes place during *chol hamoed* of Passover or Sukkot, the mourner waits until the conclusion of the festival before sitting *shivah*. One does not sit *shivah* on Purim, but Chanukah has no impact on *shivah*.

Key words and phrases:

Kaddishel קַדִישְׁל (Yiddish). "Little *Kaddish*." An affectionate diminutive applied by parents to a child as an expression of their expectation that someday, when they die, he or she will say *Kaddish* for them.

Seudat ha'havra'ah סְעוּדַת הַהַבְרָאָה. Meal of condolence prepared by friends and offered as the first meal after mourners return from the cemetery.

Sheloshim שְׁלוֹשִׁים. Literally "thirty"; the first thirty days of mourning (*shivah* plus the twenty-three days that follow).

Shivah שִׁבְעָה. First seven days of mourning.

If you want to know more:

Ronald H. Isaacs and Kerry M. Olitzky, *A Jewish Mourner's Handbook* (Hoboken, NJ, 1991).

Ron Wolfson, *A Time to Mourn, a Time to Comfort* (New York, 1993).

More particulars:

1. Round-shaped foods (eggs, chickpeas) which reflect the circle of life are often served at the meal of condolence.

2. Traditionally, the mourner is encouraged to lead services in the house of *shivah* (providing he or she is able to do so).

3. In Sephardic homes, it is traditional for mourners to sit on pillows or on the floor in a house of *shivah*. In addition, mourners study the *Zohar* (the primary source for Jewish mysticism) during the week of *shivah*.

4. When counting days of *shivah*, a part of a day counts for a whole day.

How to Write a Condolence Letter
נֶחֱמָתָא

The source:

"After the death of Abraham, God visited and blessed Isaac, his son" (Genesis 25:11). In this verse, God comforts Isaac. As a result, the rabbis teach us that it is our religious obligation to comfort the bereaved.

What you need to know:

1. Comforting the mourner is considered a supreme act of kindness in Judaism.

2. While one makes a short visit to the mourner at the house of shivah, this in not always possible. Thus, writing a letter of condolence is also greatly appreciated by the bereaved.

Here are some suggestions for writing meaningful condolence letters:

a. Express your inner feelings by using words of sympathy that express your sorrow. Avoid cliches and truisms. Speak from the heart.
b. Note your personal memories of the deceased, reflecting the impact that he or she had on your life. Mention any outstanding qualities of him/her that you will always cherish.
c. Remind the mourner that you will always "be there" for them, that they are not alone in their grief.
d. Conclude your letter with some words of love and the traditional greeting to mourners which is "May God comfort you among the other mourners of Zion and Jerusalem."

Key words and phrases:

Hamakom yenachem otcha (m), *otach* (f) *betoch she'ar aveilay tzion ve'yerushalayim:* הַמָּקוֹם יְנַחֵם אוֹתְךָ (אוֹתָךְ) בְּתוֹךְ

85

שְׁאָר אֲבֵלֵי צִיּוֹן וִירוּשָׁלְָיִם "May God comfort you among the other mourners of Zion and Jerusalem," traditional greeting to mourners, at the end of an interment and when they return to the synagogue on Shabbat during shiva.

If you want to know more:

Sidney Greenberg, *A Treasury of Comfort.* (Los Angeles, 1960).

Ronald H. Isaacs and Kerry M. Olitzky, *A Jewish Mourner's Handbook.* (Hoboken, NJ, 1991).

Barbara Fortgang Summers, *Community Responsibility in the Jewish Tradition.* (New York, 1978).

How to Prepare an Ethical Will
צַוָּאָה מוּסָרִית

The source:

While there is no specific source for the practice of writing ethical wills, many examples of parents offering final words of guidance to their children are available, such as the deathbed statement of Jacob to his sons in Genesis 49. Many of the medieval ethical wills use the Book of Proverbs as a source for practical advice on how to lead a good life.

What you need to know:

1. The sole aim of the ethical will is to provide the recipient with guidance for behavior. So don't worry about a theoretical core. For once, it is unnecessary.

2. You may want to secure your ethical will and ask that it not be read until after your death. Some people, however, want to discuss the will's contents with their children before their death. Whether or not to do so depends in part on the age of one's children.

3. Some people use milestone events like a significant birthday or major life challenges like surviving an illness or the death of an elderly parent to revise their ethical wills.

4. Feel free to put your ethical will on audiotape or videotape. As technological advances are made, you may want to use other means as well.

5. As a beginning, review the major events or accomplishments in your life and what you have learned from them. Include insights, practical advice, and ethical decisions you have made.

6. The ethical will may be included in your regular will. Remember to include *tzedakah*.

87

Things to remember:

The goal of the ethical will is to provide those who come after you with sound advice based on what you have learned from life. In other words, you want them to be able to learn what you have learned without having to experience some of the challenges you had to face.

Key words and phrases:

Hanhagot הַנְהָגוֹת. Guidance manuals for everyday living from the medieval period.

Musar מוּסָר. Classic form of ethical guidance from Jewish tradition.

Tzava'ah צַוָּאָה. Will, instruction.

If you want to know more:

Israel Abrahams, *Hebrew Ethical Wills* (Philadelphia, 1926).
Jacob Rader Marcus, *This I Believe* (Northvale, NJ, 1991).
Jack Reimer and Nathaniel Stampfer, *So That Your Values Live On: Ethical Wills and How to Prepare Them* (Woodstock, VT, 1991).

More particulars:

In addition to its personal impact on family members, the ethical will had great influence as a literary genre. Thus, major works have been written in the form of a parent writing to a child, for example.

How to Write a Living Will
צַוָּאַת חַיִּים

The sources:

1. "A dying person is considered as a living person in all matters. It is forbidden to touch the person to prevent the hastening of death" (Code of Jewish Law, Yoreh Deah 339:1).

2. "Even if a patient has agonized for a long time, it is forbidden to hasten death by, for instance, closing his eyes or removing a pillow from under his head" (ibid.).

3. "If there is an obstacle which prevents the departure of the soul, such as noise outside or salt present on the dying person's tongue, we may stop the noise or remove the salt in order not to hinder death" (ibid., commentary of Rabbi Moses Isserles).

What you need to know:

1. Jewish law obliges us to care for our bodies in the best way possible, since we are made in the image of God. Similarly, it allows for and permits a person who has a life-threatening illness to prepare for a death with dignity.

2. Directives called living wills tell doctors, hospital staff, or nursing home employees whether you want to be kept alive on artificial life-support systems if you are in a coma beyond all reasonable hope for recovery. Laws concerning advanced directives for health care vary in different states and countries, so inquire about the law in your state when deciding what to do. In addition, each Jewish religious movement has developed its own Jewish medical directive for health care, in accordance with its own interpretation of Jewish laws and values. This directive will guide you and family members in making the appropriate decisions.

3. Jewish living wills should include the following:

   a. Goals of the medical treatment.
   b. Knowledge of the person's medical condition.

c. Appointment of a health care agent.
d. Rabbinic consultation.
e. Modes of feeding if terminally ill.
f. Use of so-called aggressive medical procedures, including mechanical life support.
g. Use of cardiopulmonary resuscitation.
h. Type of pain relief.
i. Choice of hospital or home care.
j. Wishes in case of death, including organ donation and autopsy.

Things to remember:

1. It is advisable to talk over the matter of a living will with your physician and your rabbi so that all of the relevant medical facts and Jewish law can be explained to you.

2. It is advisable to secure a durable power of attorney that names someone to carry out your wishes.

3. Once you have completed a living will, you should give a copy of your document appointing a proxy to the close members of your family. You may also wish to carry a card in your wallet or purse indicating that you have appointed a proxy and telling how that person can be contacted.

Sample Living Will from the Euthanasia Educational Council:

To my family, my physician, my lawyer, my clergyperson,
To any medical facility in whose care I happen to be,
To any individual who may become responsible for my health, welfare, or affairs:

Death is as much a reality as birth, growth, maturity, and old age—it is the one certainty of life. If the time comes when I, _____, can no longer take part in decisions for my own future, let this statement stand as an expression of my wishes, while I am still of sound mind.

If the situation should arise in which there is no reasonable expectation of my recovery from physical or mental disability, I request that I be allowed to die and not be kept alive by artificial means or "heroic measures." I do not fear death itself as much as the indignities of deterioration, dependence, and hopeless pain. I therefore ask that medication be mercifully administered to me to alleviate suffering even though this may hasten the moment of death.

This request is made after careful consideration. I hope you who care for me will feel morally bound to follow its mandate. I recognize that this appears to place a heavy responsibility upon you, but it is with the intention of relieving you of such responsibility and of placing it upon myself in accordance with my strong convictions, that this statement is made.

Signed _____

Date _____

Witness _____

Witness _____

Copies of this request have been given to _____

_____

Sample Durable Power of Attorney for Health Care Appointment of Proxy form:

My name: _____

I am over eighteen years old and of sound mind. Should I become medically unable to make health care decisions for myself, I name _____, my _____, (relationship) as my representative to make medical decisions for me. S/he resides at _____, where the telephone number is _____.

Signature of designated proxy: _____

Notary's seal and signature

Dated: _____

4. A copy of your appointment of proxy should be given to your physician, proxy, and family, and a copy of your living will to your proxy. Two witnesses should sign the document in the presence of a notary.

Key words and phrases:

Living will. Document that tells doctors and hospital staff what medical directives to follow when a person is in a coma beyond any reasonable hope of recovery.

Proxy. Authority or power to act on behalf of another person.

If you want to know more:

Richard Address, *A Time to Prepare: A Practical Guide for Individuals and Families in Extraordinary Medical Treatment and Financial Arrangements* (Philadelphia, 1991).

Elliot N. Dorff, "Choose Life: A Jewish Perspective on Medical Ethics," vol. 4, no. 1 *University Papers.* The University of Judaism (Los Angeles, 1985).

Aaron Mackler, ed., *Jewish Medical Directives for Health Care* (New York, 1994).

James L. Simon, Raymond Zwerin, and Audrey Friedman Marcus, *Bioethics: A Jewish View* (Denver, 1984).

Saying Yizkor
יִזְכּוֹר

The Source:

The custom may date back to the period of the Maccabees (ca. 165 B.C.E.), when Judah and his men prayed for the souls of their fallen companions and brought offerings to the Temple in Jerusalem in order to atone for the sins of the dead.

What you need to know:

1. While there is a traditional three-part framework for the memorial service, the specific texts read may differ in some synagogues. In general, the *Yizkor* service begins with a prayer asking God to remember particular individuals (*Yizkor Elohim,* "May God remember . . ."), framed by biblical passages related to the meaning of life and death. Some congregations expand the material; others limit it. As is the practice in many synagogues today, you may want to add material which reflects the lives of Jewish martyrs and those who perished in the Holocaust. Next, chant *El Malei Rachamim,* in which we ask God to shelter the souls of our loved ones, and end with the *Av Ha'rachamim* prayer before returning the Torah to the ark. In Conservative and Reform synagogues, the Mourner's *Kaddish* is generally recited. Some congregations also read Psalm 23. In Sephardic synagogues, the memorial prayer is recited during the Torah service and said by those individuals who are given Torah honors.

2. As with *Yahrtzeit,* it is customary to light a twenty-four hour candle on the evening preceding *Yizkor.* No special prayer is required. Consult your own *siddur* for suggested readings. Alternatively, you may want to simply speak from the heart with a prayer to God, beginning with something like, "I now remember my dear _____ who has gone to his/her eternal resting place. May his/her soul be given life everlasting, and may his/her memory be a source of blessing to those who knew and loved him/her."

93

Mourners often also make a *tzedakah* contribution or pledge some act of *gemilut chasadim* to honor the memory of their loved ones.

Things to remember:

1. Different synagogues (and their representative religious movements) have different traditions about *Yizkor* memorial services.

2. In the Ashkenazic ritual, *Yizkor* is recited after the reading of the Torah during the morning service of the last day of Passover, Shavuot, and Sukkot (Shemini Atzeret) and on Yom Kippur. In the Sephardic ritual, it is also recited on Erev Yom Kippur (Kol Nidre eve) before the *ma'ariv* (evening) service.

Key words and phrases:

Gemilut chasadim גְּמִילוּת חַסָדִים. Loving acts of kindness, often in the form of volunteerism.

Hazkarat Neshamot הַזְכָּרַת נְשָׁמוֹת. Literally, "the mentioning of individual souls"; technical name for the *Yizkor* service.

Tzedakah צְדָקָה. Charitable giving.

Yahrtzeit יָאָרצייט. Yearly anniversary, on the Hebrew calendar, of the date of death of loved ones.

Yizkor יִזְכּוֹר. Literally "May He remember," referring to God's remembrance of a particular person who has died. Among those who prefer to use gender-neutral theological terminology, this is often rendered as "May You remember" or "May God remember." Since the word *yizkor* is the opening of the principal part of the first memorial prayer recited on Yom Kippur, Shemini Atzeret, Passover, and Shavuot, *Yizkor* has come to be the designation for the entire memorial service.

Yizkor-buch יִזְכּוֹר־בּוּךְ (Yiddish). Alternatively, *memorbuch* or *kunteres*. Memorial books dating back to medieval times, listing the names of martyrs killed during Crusade-related pogroms in Jewish communities of Western and Central Europe.

If you want to know more:

Ronald H. Isaacs and Kerry M. Olitzky, *A Jewish Mourner's Handbook* (Hoboken, NJ, 1991).

More particulars:

1. Some people who have living parents choose not to participate in *Yizkor* services. For some departed, especially the millions killed in the Holocaust, there is no one left to say *Yizkor*.

2. While it is common practice not to recite *Yizkor* on the holiday following a death, one may do so. Consult your rabbi for guidance.

3. Some believe that the deeds of merit of the dead can help atone for the sins of their descendants. However, others oppose this notion and contend that only the individual's deeds count before God.

4. Some Reform congregations say *Yizkor* on the afternoon of Yom Kippur rather than in the morning as part of the Torah service.

How to Take a Dip in the *Mikvah*
מִקְוֶה

The source:

The Torah requires immersion in a *mikvah* (ritual bath) to cleanse the body from impurity resulting from leprosy, discharge of semen, menstruation, childbirth, or contact with a corpse (see Leviticus 12:2, 15:5–13; Numbers 19:19).

What you need to know:

1. From ancient times until the present the *mikvah* has played an important part in maintaining Jewish family purity (*taharat ha'mishpachah*).

2. The water of the *mikvah* has to come from a natural spring or a river, and must be running, not drawn. The *mikvah* must have a minimum of 120 gallons of water.

3. Traditionally the *mikvah* is used by women after their menstrual cycle and in certain groups by both men and women as an aid to spirituality, particularly on the eve of the Sabbath and festivals, especially the Day of Atonement. Converts (Jews by choice) are required to use the *mikvah* as part of the ceremony of conversion. (Some Reform rabbis do not require the use of the *mikvah* for conversion.)

4. The *mikvah* is also used to immerse new vessels and utensils manufactured by non-Jews (in accordance with Numbers 31:22–23).

5. At the *mikvah,* people prepare themselves for the ritual immersion by bathing or showering first and removing all articles from their bodies, such as jewelry, hairpins, and so forth. After immersing completely in the *mikvah,* women recite the following blessing:

בָּרוּךְ אַתָּה יהוה אֱלֹהֵינוּ מֶלֶךְ הָעוֹלָם, אֲשֶׁר קִדְּשָׁנוּ בְּמִצְוֹתָיו
וְצִוָּנוּ עַל הַטְּבִילָה:

Baruch atah Adonai elohaynu melech ha'olam asher kid-shanu b'mitzvotav ve'tzivanu al ha'tevillah.

Praised are You, Adonai our God, Sovereign of the Universe, who has instructed us concerning ritual immersion.

After the immersion, totally immerse yourself once again. *Note:* If you are using the *mikvah* for conversion to Judaism, immerse two additional times. Then recite the *Shehecheyanu* blessing:

בָּרוּךְ אַתָּה יהוה אֱלֹהֵינוּ מֶלֶךְ הָעוֹלָם, שֶׁהֶחֱיָנוּ וְקִיְּמָנוּ וְהִגִּיעָנוּ, לַזְּמַן הַזֶּה:

Praised are You, Adonai our God, Sovereign of the Universe, who has kept us alive, sustained us, and enabled us to reach this day.

Things to remember:

1. Generally, women who immerse after their menstrual period use the *mikvah* after sundown; others do so during the day.

2. Traditionally, a bride and bridegroom-to-be will immerse themselves in the *mikvah* (separately, of course) in anticipation of their wedding.

3. Traditional Jewish women immerse themselves in the *mikvah* after bearing a child.

Key words and phrases:

Mikvah מִקְוֶה (plural, *mikva'ot* מִקְוָאוֹת). Ritual bath.
Taharat ha'mishpachah טָהֳרַת הַמִשְׁפָּחָה. Family purity.
Tevillah טְבִילָה. Ritual immersion.

If you want to know more:

Philip Birnbaum, *A Book of Jewish Concepts* (New York, 1964).

Hayim Donin, *To Be a Jew* (New York, 1972).

Encyclopaedia Judaica (Jerusalem, 1971), 11:1534.

Ron Isaacs, *Becoming Jewish: A Handbook for Conversion* (Hoboken, NJ, 1994)

Aryeh Kaplan, *Waters of Eden: The Mystery of the Mikvah* (New York, 1982).

How to Save the Planet
גְּאוּלָה

The source:

"The earth is Adonai's and all it contains" (Psalm 24:1). Alternatively, "Generations come and go, but the earth stands forever" (Kohelet 1:4).

What you need to know:

1. The earth is not ours. We are lent the earth while we are sojourners on it. Just as we received it for our use, we must bequeath it to our children and grandchildren.

2. Judaism forbids the wanton destruction of anything. Hence the charge, "When you besiege a city for a long time, making war against it in order to take it, you shall not destroy (*bal tashchit*) its trees by yielding an axe against them. You shall not cut them down" (Deuteronomy 20:19).

3. The Torah sets aside a sabbatical year—and a jubilee—for the earth to rest. Some form of crop rotation might be a modern take on this practice.

Things to remember:

1. Shabbat helps us to remember our responsibility to the world.

2. Recycle—even when it requires an extra effort or seems more expensive to do so.

3. Whenever possible, don't replace—repair.

4. Be an advocate. When you see people abusing the earth, gently remind them of their responsibility to those who come after us.

5. Famous for its Blue Boxes, the Jewish National Fund helps us to restore and protect the land of Israel. It plants forests, prepares the soil, builds roads through mountains and deserts, and gives land and employment

to new immigrants. JNF is also active in the race to harness solar energy.

Key words and phrases:

Bal tashchit בַּל תַּשְׁחִית. Mitzvah which prohibits the willful and wanton destruction of anything from which someone might benefit, especially living things.

Chag Ha'ilanot חַג הָאִילָנוֹת. Holiday of the trees, Tu Bishevat.

Shmittah שְׁמִיטָה. Sabbatical year.

Yovel יוֹבֵל. Jubilee year, occurring every half-century.

If you want to know more:

Ellen Bernstein and Dan Fink, *Let the Earth Teach You* (Wyncote, PA, 1992).

John Javna, *50 Simple Things Kids Can Do to Save the Earth* (Kansas City, 1990).

Yaakov Kirschen, *Trees, the Green Testament* (New York, 1993).

Mary Ann F. Kohl and Cindy Gainer, *Good Earth Art: Environment Art for Kids* (Bellingham, Wa, 1991).

Lillan Ross, *The Judaic Roots of Ecology* (Miami, 1986).

Jeffrey Schrier, *Judaism and Ecology* (Washington, DC, and Wyncote, PA, 1993).

More particulars:

1. As an excellent Bar/Bat Mitzvah project, we recommend that students commit themselves to three things: (a) a program that feeds the hungry and houses the homeless; (b) an act of *gemilut chasadim* that makes the world a better place to live in, which can include simple things like a litter patrol; and (c) time and *tzedakah* to protect wildlife and endangered animals (as well as those that could possibly be threatened in the future with endangerment).

2. Many people associate Jewish work toward saving the planet as part of an effort to repair a broken world (*tikkun olam*). Others relate it to celebrating the festival of Tu Bishevat, but most Jewish holidays have some explicit connection to the land.

Avoiding the Evil Eye
עַיִן הָרַע

The source:

In Pirke Avot, the rabbis teach that a good eye (by which they mean generosity) is the best quality of a person. On the other hand, an "evil eye" is the worst quality. In time, it became a widespread belief that a malevolent glance could actually work evil on the person at whom it was directed. As a result, according to the Babylonian Talmud (Baba Metzia 107b), ninety-nine people out of a hundred died of an evil eye.

What you need to know:

1. Belief in a potentially evil power residing in the eye is widespread in human culture.

2. In early Jewish sources "evil eye" simply denoted envy of the good fortune of another person. For example, "The one who has an evil eye hastens after riches" (Proverbs 28:22).

3. In talmudic times, it was believed that the evil eye could not harm a descendant of Joseph (Babylonian Talmud, Berachot 55b). Hence, we find the following incantation to ward off the evil eye: "Take the thumb of the right hand in the left hand, and the thumb of the left hand in the right hand, and say: 'I, so-and-so, am of the seed of Joseph, over which the evil eye has no power.'"

4. Over the centuries, various amulets (such as the *chamsa,* an amulet that looks like a hand, often containing an eye in its center), charms, and spells to ward off the evil eye have been developed and used. Here are several examples:

   a. Tie a red band around the wrist of a newborn child to avert the spell of the evil eye.
   b. If a woman is childless, she should find an *etrog* after the holiday of Sukkot and bite the tip off it.
   c. Use candles at a wedding ceremony to ward off the evil eye.

d. When a husband gives the evil eye to his wife (or vice versa), it will be removed if she opens her hand and says *chamesh* (five).

e. A loud *shofar* blast can be used to drive away the evil eye.

f. To prevent a bad dream, put a prayer book under your pillow.

Things to remember:

1. If someone praises your good health or good fortune, use the Hebrew words *blee ayin hara* ("without a begrudging eye") or the Yiddish phrase *kenanhora* (a collapsed form of "like an evil eye") to ward off the evil spirits.

2. In modern times, the use of paint, generally on building or on the walls of interior rooms, and metal amulets in the form of an open palm of the hand, are popular ways of avoiding the evil eye.

3. Spitting or saying "pooh pooh pooh" is considered a potent means of warding off the evil eye, especially among Eastern European immigrants.

4. Always be sure not to accept a Torah *aliyah* immediately before or after one of your blood relatives. In this way, you will avoid the evil eye.

Key words and phrases:

Blee ayin hara בְּלִי עַיִן הָרָע. Literally, "without a begrudging eye."

Kenanhora קֵיין עַיִן־הָרָע/קֵיינֶען־הָרָע (Yiddish). "Like an evil eye"; as in "Don't give him/her a *kenanhora*."

If you want to know more:

Louis Jacobs, *What Does Judaism Say About . . . ?* (Jerusalem, 1973).

Brenda Z. Rosenbaum, *How to Avoid the Evil Eye* (New York, 1985).

Rivka Ulmer, *The Evil Eye in the Bible and Rabbinic Literature* (Hoboken, NJ, 1994).

Doing *Teshuvah*
תְּשׁוּבָה

The source:

"Repent on the day before you die" (Pirke Avot 2:10).

What you need to know:

1. While *teshuvah* specifically means turning or returning to a life of Torah and *mitzvot,* it refers generally to the process of getting one's life back in order.

2. *Teshuvah* requires constant attention through study, prayer, and good acts. Begin with yourself (through the process of introspection called *cheshbon ha'nefesh*), then focus on your relationships with others. Start by avoiding gossip, going to *shul* regularly, and studying.

Things to remember:

1. It takes only one step to turn and face the other direction in life.

2. *Teshuvah* is an ongoing, lifelong process. You never really finish the process of turning. That's its power and its mystery.

3. Use the opportunities provided to you in the Jewish calendar, such as Yom Kippur, to do *teshuvah.* Use the month of Elul (usually late August–early September) as a period of introspection prior to the High Holy Day period. Recite Psalm 27 each day as a means of directing your thoughts.

Key words and phrases:

Cheshbon ha'nefesh חֶשְׁבּוֹן הַנֶּפֶשׁ. Literally, "accounting of the soul"; life review, introspection.
Teshuvah תְּשׁוּבָה. Literally, "turning" or "returning" to God and a life of goodness; repentance.

If you want to know more:

Leonard S. Kravitz and Kerry M. Olitzky, *The Journey of the Soul: Traditional Sources on Teshuvah* (Northvale, NJ, 1995).

Lawrence S. Kushner, *The Book of Words* (Woodstock, VT, 1994).

____ and Kerry M. Olitzky, *Sparks Beneath the Surface: A Spiritual Commentary on the Torah* (Northvale, NJ, 1994).

Kerry M. Olitzky, *100 Blessings Every Day* (Woodstock, VT, 1994).

More particulars:

For some, *teshuvah* is part of a process of recovery from addiction or some other compulsive behavior. For others, it is a means of getting their lives back in order. While your soul needs a healthy place to reside, it should be kept "clean" for its own sake. Therefore, stop abusing your body with alcohol and other drugs. Exercise and watch what you eat.

How to Be a *Mentsch*
מֶענְטְש

The source:

"In a place where people do not act like human beings, strive to be one [i.e., strive to be a *mentsch*]" (Pirke Avot 2:6).

What you need to know:

1. Treat others as you would want to be treated. This is the essential ingredient of being a *mentsch*. As Rabbi Hillel said, "What is hateful to you, do not do to someone else." (Babylonian Talmud, Shabbat 31a).

Things to remember:

Martin Buber, the noted theologian, suggested that our relationship with others should mirror our relationship with God.

Key words and phrases:

Mentsch מֶענְטְש (Yiddish). A good person, a "human" person.

Mentschlichkeit מֶענְטְשלֶעכְקייט (Yiddish). The quality or state of being a *mentsch*.

If you want to know more:

Neil Kurshan, *How to Be a Mentsch* (New York, 1992).

More particulars:

Being a *mentsch* is indispensable in our struggle to bring the *mashiach* (Messiah) into the world. When we turn strangers into friends, then there is real potential for ultimate peace in the world.

How to Bring the *Mashiach*
מָשִׁיחַ

The source:

According to Jewish tradition, God chose King David and his descendants, when David was at the height of his power, to reign over Israel to the end of time (see II Samuel 7; 23:1–3, 5; 22:44–51). This was the beginning of what has come to be known as the Messiah (*mashiach*) and the messianic era.

What you need to know:

1. Originally the word *mashiach* (meaning "anointed one") referred to anointed kings and high priests. These humans had a special mission from God.

2. After the Babylonian exile (586 B.C.E.) prophets had visions of the universal establishment of God's sovereignty under a scion of King David's house, who would be God's anointed. This individual would bring total and complete peace to the world and spiritual regeneration to all humanity.

3. Jewish tradition described Elijah the Prophet as the forerunner of the Messiah.

4. Jewish tradition contains numerous references to the Messiah. Here are some which suggest ways in which you may hasten the coming of the Messiah:

> a. "The Messiah will come when the entire Jewish people keep two Sabbaths in a row" (Babylonian Talmud, Shabbat 118b). In order to help, you may want to consider increasing your personal Sabbath observance.
>
> b. "If you are planting a tree and you hear that the Messiah has come, first finish planting the tree and then run to the city gates to greet the Messiah" (Yochanan ben Zakkai in Leviticus Rabbah 25:3). To respond to this text, do what you can to preserve the ecological balance of the world.

c. "In the time of the Messiah, nation shall not lift up sword against nation; neither shall people know war anymore" (Isaiah 2:4). To extend the meaning of this message, do all that you can to promote peace in the world.

d. "On that day God shall be One and God's name shall be One" (Zechariah 14:9). The word "one" (*echad*) is an integral part of the *Shema* prayer. Say the *Shema* every morning and evening, and as you pronounce *echad*, concentrate on the concept of God's Oneness.

e. Rabbi Joshua ben Levi found Elijah the Prophet, disguised as a leper, begging at the gates of Rome. "When will you come to proclaim the Messiah? " he asked. "Today, if you will hear his voice," replied Elijah (Babylonian Talmud, Sanhedrin 98a). Therefore, listen carefully to the Messiah's voice, especially at times when the name of Elijah is invoked (as at a circumcision ceremony, or at the Passover *seder,* and at the *Havdalah* ceremony bidding farewell to the Sabbath on Saturday evenings).

f. "In the days of the Messiah there will be no hunger or war, no jealousy or strife; prosperity will be universal, and the world's predominant occupation will be to know God" (Code of Jewish Law, Melachim 12:2, 5). Therefore, try to do all you can to feed the hungry and not cause strife or jealousy among your family and friends.

Key words and phrases:

Mashiach מָשִׁיחַ. Literally "one who is anointed"; now used specifically in reference to the Messiah.

If you want to know more:

Philip Birnbaum, *A Book of Jewish Concepts* (New York, 1964).
Encyclopaedia Judaica (Jerusalem, 1971), 11:1407–1416.

More particulars:

1. Throughout Jewish history many people have claimed to be the Messiah. They are called "false messiahs." Shab-

batai Tzvi (1626–1676), who proclaimed himself Messiah in 1648, was the most notorious.

2. An alternative Jewish tradition (which surfaces in the midrash) suggests that the messianic line can be traced through Joseph rather than David.

2. Some Jews, generally those affiliated with the Reform and Reconstructionist movements, believe that the messianic era will be ushered in, not by a single individual known as the Messiah, but by the cumulative activities of the entire Jewish people.

Instant Information
Angels and Demons

What you need to know:

In Jewish tradition, God is often considered to delegate power to a messenger or angels directed to perform God's will. Demons are also considered messengers of God, but their role was to bring harm to people. Here is a partial summary of some of the more well known angels and demons in Jewish tradition.

Ashmodai. Destructive angel and king of the demons. His name means "Destroyer."

Beelzebub. Sovereign of the netherworld. His name means "Lord of the Flies."

Cherubim. Angelic sentinels who guarded the Tree of Life in the Garden of Eden. Statues of cherubim adorned the Tabernacle and later the Temple in Jerusalem.

Gabriel. Leader of the archangels; one of the two angels mentioned by name in the Bible (Daniel 8:10).

Lilith. Female demon who reigned at night; often considered the queen of the demons.

Malach ha'mavet. Angel of Death, charged with summoning dying souls from the earth.

Metatron. In mystical literature, the highest figure in the angelic world.

Michael. One of the two angels mentioned by name in the Bible (Daniel 8:10).

Ophanim. Angelic drivers of the holy chariot, as depicted in the Book of Ezekiel; their name means "Wheels."

Raphael. One of seven archangels who brought prayers before God; his name means "God heals."

Raziel. Angel of magic; his name means "Secret of God."

Samael. Prince of the evil demons.

Satan. As in the Book of Job, the accuser who called God's attention to people's sins; his name means "Adversary."

Seraphim. In Isaiah 6:2 these "fiery angels" declare God's holiness.

Uriel. Prince of the archangels; identified by thunder and earthquakes.

If you want to know more:

Morris B. Margolies, *A Gathering of Angels: Angels in Jewish Life and Literature* (New York, 1994).

Instant Information
The Twenty-third Psalm
תְּהִלִים כ"ג

The source:

Jewish tradition attributes the composition of the Twenty-third Psalm and much of the Book of Psalms to King David.

What you need to know:

מִזְמוֹר לְדָוִד. יהוה רֹעִי לֹא אֶחְסָר: בִּנְאוֹת דֶּשֶׁא יַרְבִּיצֵנִי. עַל
מֵי מְנוּחוֹת יְנַהֲלֵנִי: נַפְשִׁי יְשׁוֹבֵב. יַנְחֵנִי בְמַעְגְּלֵי צֶדֶק לְמַעַן
שְׁמוֹ: גַּם כִּי אֵלֵךְ בְּגֵיא צַלְמָוֶת לֹא אִירָא רָע. כִּי אַתָּה עִמָּדִי.
שִׁבְטְךָ וּמִשְׁעַנְתֶּךָ הֵמָּה יְנַחֲמֻנִי: תַּעֲרֹךְ לְפָנַי שֻׁלְחָן נֶגֶד צֹרְרָי.
דִּשַּׁנְתָּ בַשֶּׁמֶן רֹאשִׁי. כּוֹסִי רְוָיָה: אַךְ טוֹב וָחֶסֶד יִרְדְּפוּנִי כָּל יְמֵי
חַיָּי. וְשַׁבְתִּי בְּבֵית יהוה לְאֹרֶךְ יָמִים:

Adonai is my shepherd, I lack nothing.
God gives me my rest near rich pastures.
God leads me beside tranquil waters to revive my spirit.
God guides me on straight paths, for that is God's nature.
Though I walk through the valley of the shadows
I fear no evil, for You are with me.
Your sustaining staff comforts me.
You permit me to eat in the presence of my enemies.
You anoint my head with oil, my cup runs over.
Surely goodness and mercy will accompany me for the rest of my life.
And I will spend my days in God's court forever.

Mizmor L'David
Adonai ro'ee lo echsar
Beenot desheh yarbeetzaynee
Al may menuchot yenahalaynee nafshee yeshovayv
Yancheelaynee vemaglay tzedek le'ma'an shemo

111

Gam kee aylaych begay tzalmavet
Lo eera rah kee atah eemadee
Sheevticha u'meeshantecha haymah yenachamoonee
Ta'aroch lefanai shulchan neged tzorirai
Deeshanta vashemen roshee kosee revayah
Ach tov va'chesed yeerdefoonee kol yemai chayai
Veshavtee bevayt Adonai le'orech yameem.

Things to remember:

1. The Twenty-third Psalm expresses the most intimate, personal relationship of a person with God. It begins with the comforting metaphor of God as Shepherd, focusing God's concern for the world in the image of a shepherd for the flock.

2. Because of its message of comfort, officiants often read the Twenty-third Psalm aloud at funerals.

3. The Twenty-third Psalm may also be recited when visiting a cemetery.

Key words and phrases:

Kosee revaya. כּוֹסִי רְוָיָה My cup runs over.
Ro'ee. רֹעִי Shepherd.
Tov va-chesed. טוֹב וָחֶסֶד Goodness and mercy.

If you want to know more:

A. Cohen, *The Soncino Book of Psalms* (London, 1962).
Mitchell Dahood, *The Anchor Bible, Psalms 1–50* (New York, 1965).

Instant Information
Mourner's *Kaddish*
קַדִּישׁ יָתוֹם

The source:

Originally, the *Kaddish* was used as a short prayer at the close of sermons. At a later period the *Kaddish* was introduced into the liturgy to mark the conclusion of specific sections of the service. Since the merit of studying Torah was considered very important, the rabbis felt that one might honor the memory of the deceased through Torah study. Hence, such study was assigned to mourners. Study sessions were concluded by the chanting of the *Kaddish* (Soferim 19:12). The first official mention of the custom of the Mourner's *Kaddish* at the end of the service is found in *Or Zarua,* a thirteenth-century work of Jewish law. Rabbi Moses Isserles spoke of the "custom" of reciting the *Kaddish* for a period of eleven months after the death of a father or mother (*Shulchan Aruch,* Yoreh Deah 376:4).

What you need to know:

יִתְגַּדַּל וְיִתְקַדַּשׁ שְׁמֵהּ רַבָּא. בְּעָלְמָא דִּי בְרָא כִרְעוּתֵהּ וְיַמְלִיךְ
מַלְכוּתֵהּ. בְּחַיֵּיכוֹן וּבְיוֹמֵיכוֹן וּבְחַיֵּי דְכָל בֵּית יִשְׂרָאֵל. בַּעֲגָלָא
וּבִזְמַן קָרִיב וְאִמְרוּ אָמֵן:
יְהֵא שְׁמֵהּ רַבָּא מְבָרַךְ לְעָלַם וּלְעָלְמֵי עָלְמַיָּא:
יִתְבָּרַךְ וְיִשְׁתַּבַּח וְיִתְפָּאַר וְיִתְרוֹמַם וְיִתְנַשֵּׂא וְיִתְהַדָּר וְיִתְעַלֶּה
וְיִתְהַלָּל שְׁמֵהּ דְּקוּדְשָׁא. בְּרִיךְ הוּא. לְעֵלָּא (בעשי״ת וּלְעֵלָּא
מִכָּל) מִן כָּל בִּרְכָתָא וְשִׁירָתָא. תֻּשְׁבְּחָתָא וְנֶחֱמָתָא. דַּאֲמִירָן
בְּעָלְמָא. וְאִמְרוּ אָמֵן:
יְהֵא שְׁלָמָא רַבָּא מִן שְׁמַיָּא וְחַיִּים עָלֵינוּ וְעַל כָּל יִשְׂרָאֵל וְאִמְרוּ
אָמֵן. עוֹשֶׂה שָׁלוֹם בִּמְרוֹמָיו הוּא יַעֲשֶׂה שָׁלוֹם עָלֵינוּ וְעַל כָּל
יִשְׂרָאֵל וְאִמְרוּ אָמֵן:

Yit-ga-dal ve-yit-ka-dash she-mei ra-ba be-al-ma di-ve-ra chi-re-u-tei, ve-yam-lich mal-chu-tei be-cha-yei-chon u-ve-yo-mei-chon u-ve-cha-yei de-chol beit Yis-ra-eil, ba-a-ga-la u-vi-ze-man ka-riv ve-i-me-ru: a-mein.

Ye-hei she-mai ra-ba me-va-rach le-a-lam u-le-al-mei al-ma-ya.

Yit-ba-rach ve-yish-ta-bach, ve-yit-pa-ar ve-yit-ro-mam ve-yit-na-sei ve-yit-ha-dar ve-yit-a-leh ve-yit-ha-lal she-mei de-ku-de-sha be-rich hu le-ei-la min kol bi-re-cha-ta ve-shi-ra-ta tush-be-cha-ta ve-ne-che-ma-ta da-ami-ran be-al-ma ve-i-me-ru a-mein.

Ye-hei she-la-ma ra-ba min she-ma-ya ve-cha-yim a-lei-nu ve-al kol Yis-ra-eil ve-i-me-ru a-mein.

O-seh sha-lom bi-me-ro-mav hu ya-a-seh sha-lom a-lei-nu ve-al kol Yis-ra-eil ve-i-me-ru a-mein.

Let the glory of God be extolled, let God's great name be hallowed, in the world whose creation God willed. May God's sovereignty soon prevail, in our own day, our own lives, and the life of all Israel, and let us say Amen.

Let God's great name be blessed for ever and ever.

Let the name of God be glorified, exalted, and honored, though God is beyond all the praises, songs, and adorations that we can utter, and let us say Amen.

For us and for all Israel, may the blessing of peace and the promise of life come true, and let us say Amen.

May God, who causes peace to reign in the high heavens, let peace descend on us, on all Israel, and all the world, and let us say: Amen.

Things to remember:

1. The *Kaddish* is traditionally said in a *minyan* (prayer quorum) of ten persons. (Reform Judaism does not require a *minyan.*)

2. Traditionally, one is required to say *Kaddish* for deceased parents. The Conservative, Reform, and Reconstructionist movements have come to understand this obligation as binding on daughters as well as on sons.

3. While not required, most communities encourage the recitation of *Kaddish* for other deceased relatives, including brother, sister, son, daughter, husband and wife.

4. The Mourner's *Kaddish* may be recited for anyone, especially close friends, martyrs, Torah scholars, soldiers, and anyone who died for the sanctification of God's name.

5. The Mourner's *Kaddish* is said while standing.

6. The Mourner's *Kaddish* functions differently than the other *Kaddish* prayers (such as the reader's or half-Kaddish, used to designate different parts of the service). *Kaddish* is to be said, during the year of mourning, on Yahrtzeits, and during Yizkor memorial services.

Key words and phrases:

Kaddish Yatom. קַדִּישׁ יָתוֹם (Aramaic). Literally, "Orphan's Sanctification"; the special *Kaddish* said during the year of mourning.

If you want to know more:

Ronald H. Isaacs and Kerry M. Olitzky, *A Jewish Mourner's Handbook* (Hoboken, NJ, 1991).
Maurice Lamm, *The Jewish Way in Death and Mourning* (New York, 1972).

Instant Information
Hallel Psalms
הַלֵּל

The source:

In the Babylonian Talmud (Pesachim 117a), we learn that the prophets told the people to offer hymns of praise to God whenever we celebrate historical events that commemorate the deliverance of our people from dire straits. Today, the *Hallel* psalms of praise (Psalms 113–118) are customarily recited following the morning *Amidah* on the festivals of Passover, Shavuot, Sukkot, Chanukkah, and Rosh Chodesh. They are also often recited on Yom Ha-atzma'ut (Israel Independence Day) and on Yom Yerushalayim (Jerusalem Day).

What you need to know:

Recite the blessing before saying the *Hallel* Psalms:

בָּרוּךְ אַתָּה יהוה אֱלֹהֵינוּ מֶלֶךְ הָעוֹלָם, אֲשֶׁר קִדְּשָׁנוּ בְּמִצְוֹתָיו וְצִוָּנוּ לִקְרֹא אֶת־הַהַלֵּל.

Baruch atah Adonai elohaynu melech ha'olam asher kidshanu b'mitzvotav v'tzivanu likro et ha-Hallel.

Praised are You, Adonai our God, Sovereign of the Universe, who has made us holy through *mitzvot* and instructed us to read the *Hallel*.

Psalm 113

הַלְלוּיָהּ. הַלְלוּ, עַבְדֵי יהוה, הַלְלוּ אֶת־שֵׁם יהוה.
יְהִי שֵׁם יהוה מְבֹרָךְ מֵעַתָּה וְעַד־עוֹלָם.
מִמִּזְרַח־שֶׁמֶשׁ עַד־מְבוֹאוֹ מְהֻלָּל שֵׁם יהוה.
רָם עַל כָּל־גּוֹיִם יהוה, עַל הַשָּׁמַיִם כְּבוֹדוֹ.
מִי כַּיהוה אֱלֹהֵינוּ, הַמַּגְבִּיהִי לָשָׁבֶת,
הַמַּשְׁפִּילִי לִרְאוֹת בַּשָּׁמַיִם וּבָאָרֶץ.
מְקִימִי מֵעָפָר דָּל, מֵאַשְׁפֹּת יָרִים אֶבְיוֹן,

116

לְהוֹשִׁיבִי עִם־נְדִיבִים, עִם נְדִיבֵי עַמּוֹ.
מוֹשִׁיבִי עֲקֶרֶת הַבַּיִת, אֵם־הַבָּנִים שְׂמֵחָה. הַלְלוּיָהּ.

Halleluyah! Praise Adonai, you who serve Adonai, praise the name of Adonai.

May Adonai's name be blessed now and forever.

From sunrise to sunset, Adonai's name is praised. Adonai is above all the nations, God's glory goes beyond the heavens.

Who is like Adonai our God, who is far above us, yet bends down to look at the heavens and the earth? God lifts up the poor from the dust, The needy from the trash heap, and seats them with the nobles of God's people.

God makes the childless woman a mother happy with her children. Halleluyah!

Psalm 114

בְּצֵאת יִשְׂרָאֵל מִמִּצְרָיִם, בֵּית יַעֲקֹב מֵעַם לֹעֵז.
הָיְתָה יְהוּדָה לְקָדְשׁוֹ, יִשְׂרָאֵל מַמְשְׁלוֹתָיו.
הַיָּם רָאָה וַיָּנֹס, הַיַּרְדֵּן יִסֹּב לְאָחוֹר.
הֶהָרִים רָקְדוּ כְאֵילִים, גְּבָעוֹת כִּבְנֵי צֹאן.
מַה לְּךָ הַיָּם כִּי תָנוּס, הַיַּרְדֵּן תִּסֹּב לְאָחוֹר.
הֶהָרִים תִּרְקְדוּ כְאֵילִים, גְּבָעוֹת כִּבְנֵי־צֹאן:
מִלִּפְנֵי אָדוֹן חוּלִי אָרֶץ, מִלִּפְנֵי אֱלוֹהַּ יַעֲקֹב,
הַהֹפְכִי הַצּוּר אֲגַם מָיִם, חַלָּמִישׁ לְמַעְיְנוֹ מָיִם.

*B'tzayt Yisrael mi-Mitz-ra-yim bayt Ya'akov may-am lo'ez
Hai-y'ta Ye-hu-dah l'kad-sho, Yisrael mam-sh'lo-tav.
Ha-yam ra'ah va-ya-nos, ha-Yar-den yi-sov l'achor.
Heh-ha-reem rak-du ch'ay-leem, g'va'ot kiv'nay tzon.
Ma l'cha ha-yam kee ta-nus, ha-Yar-den ti-sov l'a-chor
Heh-ha-reem tir-k'du ch'ay-leem g'va'ot kiv'nay tzon.
Mi-lif-nay adon chuli a-retz mi-lif-nay Elo-a Ya-akov
Ha-hof-chi ha-tzur a-gam ma-yim cha-la-meesh l'mai-no
ma-yim.*

When Israel went out of Egypt, The House of Jacob from a foreign people.

Judah became God's holy people, Israel became God's nation.

The sea saw and turned back, the Jordan fled.

117

The mountains jumped like rams, the hills jumped like lambs.

What is with you, sea, that you flee;
Jordan, that you turn back;
Mountains, that you jump like rams; hills like lambs?
Quake, earth, before the Ruler, before the God of Jacob,

Who turns the rock into a pool of water;
Who turns flint into fountains.

Psalm 115:1–11

Not because we deserve it, Adonai, but for Your own reasons act gloriously, for the sake of Your lovingkindness and Your truth.

Why should the nations say, "Where is their God?"
Our God is in heaven. God does as God pleases.
Their idols are just silver and gold, made by human hands.
They have mouths and can't speak, eyes but cannot see.

They have ears but can't hear, noses but can't smell.
Their hands can't feel, their feet can't walk,
They cannot speak with their throats.
Those who make them shall become like them—all who trust in them.

Israel, trust in Adonai, our help and shield.

House of Aaron, trust in Adonai, our help and our shield.
Everyone who respects Adonai, trust in Adonai,
Our help and our shield.

Psalm 115:12–18

יהוה זְכָרָנוּ יְבָרֵךְ, יְבָרֵךְ אֶת־בֵּית יִשְׂרָאֵל, יְבָרֵךְ אֶת־בֵּית אַהֲרֹן:
יְבָרֵךְ יִרְאֵי יהוה, הַקְּטַנִּים עִם־הַגְּדֹלִים: יֹסֵף יהוה עֲלֵיכֶם,
עֲלֵיכֶם וְעַל־בְּנֵיכֶם: בְּרוּכִים אַתֶּם לַיהוָה, עֹשֵׂה שָׁמַיִם וָאָרֶץ:
הַשָּׁמַיִם שָׁמַיִם לַיהוָה, וְהָאָרֶץ נָתַן לִבְנֵי־אָדָם: לֹא־הַמֵּתִים
יְהַלְלוּ־יָהּ, וְלֹא כָּל־יֹרְדֵי דוּמָה: וַאֲנַחְנוּ נְבָרֵךְ יָהּ, מֵעַתָּה וְעַד־
עוֹלָם הַלְלוּיָהּ:

Adonai z'cha-ra-nu y'va-rech, y'va-rech et bayt Yisrael,
y'va-rech et bayt A-ha-ron.
Y'va-rech yir-ay Adonai, hak'ta-neem im ha-g'do-leem.
Yo-sef Adonai a-lay-chem, a-lay-chem v'al b'nay-chem.
B'ru-cheem a-tem l'Adonai, o-seh sha-ma-yim va-a-retz.

Ha-sha-ma-yim sha-ma-yim l'Adonai,
v'ha-a-retz na-tan liv'nay a-dam.
Lo ha-me-teem y'hal'lu Yah, v'lo kol yor-day du-mah.
Va'a-nach-nu n'va-rech Yah, may-a-tah v'ad olam Hal-
leluyah.

God, remember us and bless us;
God, bless the House of Israel.
God, bless the House of Aaron;
God, bless those who respect Adonai, everyone alike.
May Adonai increase you and your children.
You are blessed by Adonai, who made heaven and
earth.
The heavens belong to Adonai,
But the earth was given to human beings.
The dead do not praise God, nor do those that death
silences.
But we will praise God now and forever. Halleluyah!

Psalm 116:12–19

How can I pay Adonai back for all God's gifts to me?
  I will lift up the cup of deliverance, and call out
Adonai's name.
I will keep my promises to Adonai, before the whole
community.
  Thank you, Adonai, for the freedom to serve You,
  for You have released me from bondage.
I will publicly keep my promises to Adonai, in the
courts of Adonai's House, in the center of Jerusalem.
Halleluyah!

Psalm 117

הַלְלוּ אֶת־יְהֹוָה כָּל־גּוֹיִם, שַׁבְּחוּהוּ כָּל־הָאֻמִּים:
כִּי גָבַר עָלֵינוּ חַסְדּוֹ, וֶאֱמֶת־יְהֹוָה לְעוֹלָם, הַלְלוּיָה:

Hall'lu et Adonai kol goyeem, shab-chu-hu kol ha-u-meem.
Kee ga-var a-lay-nu chas-do, ve-emet Adonai l'o-lam. Hal-
leluyah!

Praise Adonai, all nations; praise God, all peoples!
God's kindness overwhelms us. Adonai's truth is for-
ever.
Halleluyah!

Psalm 118

הוֹדוּ לַיהוה כִּי טוֹב, כִּי לְעוֹלָם חַסְדּוֹ.
יֹאמַר נָא יִשְׂרָאֵל, כִּי לְעוֹלָם חַסְדּוֹ.
יֹאמְרוּ־נָא בֵית אַהֲרֹן, כִּי לְעוֹלָם חַסְדּוֹ.
יֹאמְרוּ נָא יִרְאֵי יהוה, כִּי לְעוֹלָם חַסְדּוֹ.

Ho-du l'Adonai kee tov, kee l'olam chas-do.
Yo-mar na Yisrael, kee l'o-lam chas-do.
Yom-ru na vayt A-ha-ron, kee l'o-lam chas-do.
Yom-ru na yir-ay Adonai, kee l'o-lam chas-do.

Thank Adonai for being good, God's kindness lasts forever.
Let Israel say: God's kindness lasts forever.
Let the House of Aaron say: God's kindness lasts forever.
Let those who respect Adonai say: God's kindness lasts forever.

עָזִּי וְזִמְרָת יָהּ, וַיְהִי לִי לִישׁוּעָה.

O'zee v'zimrat Yah, va-y'hee lee li-shu-ah.
God is my strength and might, and has always rescued me.

קוֹל רִנָּה וִישׁוּעָה, בְּאָהֳלֵי צַדִּיקִים,
יְמִין יהוה עֹשָׂה חָיִל.
יְמִין יהוה רוֹמֵמָה, יְמִין יהוה עֹשָׂה חָיִל.

Kol ri-nah viy'shu-ah, b'o-ha-lay tza-dee-keem.
y'meen Adonai o-sah cha-yil.
Y'meen Adonai ro-me-ma, y'meen Adonai o-sah cha-yil.

The sound of joyous songs celebrating God's help is heard in the tents of the good: Adonai's right hand does mightily! Adonai's right hand is lifted up in victory! Adonai's right hand succeeds greatly!

פִּתְחוּ־לִי שַׁעֲרֵי צֶדֶק, אָבֹא בָם, אוֹדֶה יָהּ.
זֶה הַשַּׁעַר לַיהוה, צַדִּיקִים יָבֹאוּ בוֹ.

Pit-chu lee sha'aray tzeh-dek, a-vo-vam o-deh Yah.
Zeh ha-sha'ar l'Adonai, tza-dee-keem ya-vo-u vo.

Open the gates of righteousness for me. I will enter them to thank God. This is Adonai's gate, the righteous shall enter it.

אוֹדְךָ כִּי עֲנִיתָנִי, וַתְּהִי לִי לִישׁוּעָה.
אֶבֶן מָאֲסוּ הַבּוֹנִים, הָיְתָה לְרֹאשׁ פִּנָּה.
מֵאֵת יהוה הָיְתָה זֹּאת, הִיא נִפְלָאת בְּעֵינֵינוּ.
זֶה הַיּוֹם עָשָׂה יהוה, נָגִילָה וְנִשְׂמְחָה בוֹ.

Od'cha kee a-nee-ta-nee, vat'hee lee lee-shuah.
Eh-ven ma'a-su ha-bo-neem, hai'y'ta l'rosh pi-nah.
Me-et Adonai hai'y'tah zot, hee nif-lat b'ay-nay-nu.
Zeh ha-yom a-sah Adonai, na-gee-lah v'nis-m'cha vo.

I thank You for answering me and rescuing me.
The stone which the builders rejected is now the cornerstone.
This is Adonai's doing. It is wonderful in our eyes.
This is the day that Adonai has made,
Let us rejoice and be glad on it.

אָנָּא יהוה, הוֹשִׁיעָה נָּא!
אָנָּא יהוה, הוֹשִׁיעָה נָּא!
אָנָּא יהוה, הַצְלִיחָה נָא!
אָנָּא יהוה, הַצְלִיחָה נָא!

Ana Adonai hoshee'ah na. Ana Adonai hoshee'ah na.
Ana Adonai hatz-lee-cha na. Ana Adonai hatz-lee-cha na.

Please, Adonai, save us. Please, Adonai, cause us to succeed.
May we enjoy many opportunities to thank and praise You, Adonai. It is good to thank You, it is good to praise Your name. You are God forever and ever. Praised are You, Adonai, who is a Ruler praised with songs of praise.

בָּרוּךְ אַתָּה יהוה, מֶלֶךְ מְהֻלָּל בַּתִּשְׁבָּחוֹת.

Baruch atah Adonai, melech m'hu-lal batish-bah-chot.

Praised are You, Adonai O Sovereign who is acclaimed with songs of praise.

Things to remember:

1. The psalms of *Hallel* recall the festival celebrations at the ancient Jerusalem Temple. Through the *Hallel,* we express thanksgiving and joy for God's providence and concern for our people.

2. The *Hallel* psalms are never recited on Rosh Hashanah or Yom Kippur because these holidays were not intended for rejoicing. They are also not customarily said on Purim, a festival which celebrates a miracle that happened in Persia, since the redemption was only partial.

3. The first eleven verses of Psalms 115 and 116 are not recited on the last six days of Passover and on Rosh Chodesh. When *Hallel* is said without these verses, it is called the "Half *Hallel.*"

4. *Hallel* is always recited while standing because it reflects our witness to God's wondrous deeds and power.

5. *Hallel* is recited during the morning service in Ashkenazic synagogues. In Sephardic synagogues and in some Israeli congregations it is the custom to recite *Hallel* at the evening service.

6. *Hallel* is recited at the Passover *seder,* part before the meal and part after the meal. We remain seated during the recitation of *Hallel* at the *seder.*

7. Since the *Hallel* refers to the Exodus from Egypt, this series of six psalms is called the Egyptian *Hallel.*

Key words and phrases.

Chatzi Hallel. חֲצִי הַלֵּל Half *Hallel.*
Hallel. הַלֵּל Psalms of praise.
Hallel ha-Mitzri. הַלֵּל הַמִּצְרִי Egyptian *Hallel.*

If you want to know more:

Steven Brown, *Higher and Higher: Making Jewish Prayer Part of Us* (New York, 1979).
Hayim Halevy Donin, *To Pray as a Jew* (New York, 1980).

Instant Information
The Order of the Prayer Service
סֵדֶר הַתְּפִילָה

The source:

Although some form of group prayer service existed by the early days of the Second Temple (400 B.C.E.), it was Rabbi Gamliel II, head of the Sanhedrin in the first century C.E., who first systematized the liturgy. Eight hundred years later, in the eighth century C.E., Rav Amram Gaon arranged a prayer book that is most likely the source for the modern order of worship.

What you need to know:

A general overview of the structure of the major prayer services is presented below.

Evening Service (*Ma'ariv*)

Kabbalat Shabbat. Service for welcoming the Sabbath on Friday evening.

Kol Nidre. Formulaic release of vows on the eve of Yom Kippur.

Barchu. Call to prayer, set in a poetic formula.

Ha'ma'ariv Aravim. First blessing before *Shema;* God is acknowledged as the Creator of the cycles of time and brings on the evening.

Ahavat Olam. Second blessing before *Shema;* God is acknowledged for giving Israel the Torah and showing love for the people of Israel.

Shema. Statement of faith in God as One.

Ga'al Yisrael. First blessing after *Shema;* God is recognized for the redemption of Israel.

Shomer Amo Yisrael La'ad. Second blessing after *Shema;* we ask God to bring us peace and keep us safe at night.

Selection from Bible (On Shabbat: Veshamru; other texts for holidays.)

Chatzi Kaddish. Half *Kaddish.*

Amidah. Also called *Hatefillah,* "the Prayer"; series of blessings whose themes direct worshipper's thoughts during prayer.

Vayechulu and *Magen Avot.* Recited only on Shabbat, these prayers reflect the work of Creation and the Divine instruction to rest.

Kaddish Shalem. Full *Kaddish.*

Kiddush. Blessing over wine (on Sabbath and on holidays).

Aleynu. Adoration of God.

Mourner's *Kaddish.*

Yigdal or *Adon Olam.* Concluding hymn.

Morning Service (*Shacharit*)

Blessings of the Morning.

Baruch She'amar. "God spoke and the world came to be." Selected Psalms.

Yishtabach. Prayer of praise to God.

Barchu. Call to prayer, set in a poetic formula.

Yotzer Or. First blessing before *Shema;* God is recognized as the Creator of light who renews the work of creation each day.

Ahavah Rabbah. Second blessing before *Shema;* God's love for Israel is expressed in the form of the gift of Torah.

Shema. Statement of faith in God as One.

Ga'al Yisrael. Blessing after *Shema;* God is called the Redeemer of Israel.

Amidah. Also called *Ha'tefillah,* "*the* Prayer"; series of blessings whose themes direct worshipper's thoughts during prayer.

Hallel. Psalms of praise, said on Rosh Chodesh and holidays.

Chatzi Kaddish. Half *Kaddish.*

Reading of Torah Monday, Thursday, Sabbath, Rosh Chodesh, and holidays.

Musaf. Additional service for Sabbath, Rosh Chodesh, and holidays; generally eliminated by Reform movement.

Kaddish Shalem. Full *Kaddish.*

Aleynu. Adoration of God.

Mourner's *Kaddish.*

Afternoon Service (*Minchah*)

Ashray. Psalm 145.

Uvah Letziyon. Sabbath and holidays only; "There comes a redeemer" is the theme.

Chatzi Kaddish. Half *Kaddish*.

Torah reading. Sabbath and fast days only.

Chatzi Kaddish. Half *Kaddish*.

Amidah. Also called *Hatefillah*, "*the* Prayer"; series of blessings whose themes direct worshipper's thoughts during prayer.

Kaddish Shalem. Full *Kaddish*.

Aleynu. Adoration of God.

Mourner's *Kaddish*.

Things to remember:

Although the basic order and structure of the service are the same for all religious streams or movements in Judaism, customs may vary from congregation to congregation. Some prayers may be abbreviated or omitted altogether.

Key words and phrases:

Chatzi Kaddish חֲצִי קַדִּישׁ. Half *Kaddish,* used to divide small subsections of worship service.

Kabbalat Shabbat קַבָּלַת שַׁבָּת. Short service for welcoming the Sabbath which precedes full evening service.

Kaddish Shalem קַדִּישׁ שָׁלֵם. Full *Kaddish,* used to divide major sections of service.

Ma'ariv מַעֲרִיב. Evening service.

Matbe'ah shel tefillah מַטְבֵּעַ שֶׁל תְּפִילָה. Fixed structure of prayer service.

Mincha מִנְחָה. Afternoon service.

Musaf מוּסָף. Additional service on Shabbat and holidays.

Shacharit שַׁחֲרִית. Morning service.

If you want to know more:

Hayim Donin, *To Pray as a Jew* (New York, 1980).

Evelyn Garfiel, *Service of the Heart* (Northvale, NJ, 1989).

Abraham Millgram, *Jewish Worship* (Philadelphia, 1971).

More particulars:

1. In most Reform congregations, the *musaf* service, which reflects the additional sacrifice brought to the ancient Temple for Sabbaths and holidays, has been eliminated. In addition, Reform congregations generally do not use the multiplicity of *Kaddish* prayers to separate the sections of the service (such as the Full *Kaddish* before *Aleynu*).

2. The general themes that run through the worship service are: creation, revelation, redemption.

Instant Information
The Twelve Tribes of Israel
י"ב שְׁבָטִים

The source:

According to the Bible (Genesis 49), Jacob's twelve sons eventually became the twelve tribes of Israel. They were: Reuben, Simeon, Levi, Judah, Issachar, Zebulun, Joseph, Benjamin, Dan, Naphtali, Gad, and Asher. Since Moses conferred the priestly office on the tribe of Levi (without land), he transferred the property rights of Joseph to his children, Ephraim and Manasseh, to maintain the number of tribes receiving territory at twelve (a sacred number).

What you need to know:

Here is a summary of the twelve tribes of Israel, their emblems, banners, and jewels:

Name	Emblem	Banner	Jewel
Benjamin	wolf	multicolored	jasper
Dan	serpent	deep blue	jacinth
Naphtali	deer	wine color	amethyst
Asher	woman and olive tree	pearl color	beryl
Levi	*urim* and *tummim*	white, red, and black	emerald
Judah	lion	sky blue	turquoise
Issachar	donkey	black; sun and moon	sapphire
Zebulun	ship	white	amethyst
Reuben	mandrake	red	carnelian
Simeon	city of Shechem	green	topaz
Gad	encampment	gray	crystal
Ephraim	bullock	jet black	lapis lazul
Manasseh	unicorn	jet black	lapis lazul

Things to remember:

1. The nation was divided into twelve tribes during the time of the judges and the early kings.

2. Each tribe of Israel received a portion of land when the Israelites entered Canaan after the Exodus from Egypt.

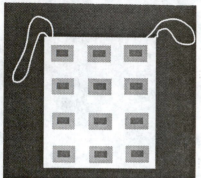

3. Although each of the tribes was "fathered" by Jacob, they had different "mothers." Leah was the mother of Reuben, Simeon, Levi, Judah, Issachar, and Zebulun. Bilhah (Rachel's maid) was the mother of Dan and Naphtali; Zilpah (Leah's maid) was the mother of Gad and Asher. Finally, Rachel was the mother of Joseph and Benjamin.

4. The tribes slowly lost their distinct identities when Israel became a more consolidated nation.

Key words and phrases:

Degel דֶּגֶל. Banner.
Shevet שֵׁבֶט. Tribe.

If you want to know more:

Nahum M. Sarna, ed., *J.P.S. Torah Commentary: Book of Genesis* (Philadelphia, 1989).

Instant Information
The *Ketubah*
כְּתוּבָה

The source:

Rabbi Shimon ben Shetach, president of the ancient rabbinic court, prepared the earliest form of the Jewish marriage contract, called a *ketubah*.

What you need to know:

1. The *ketubah* is the Jewish marriage contract that traditionally specifies the husband's primary obligations to his spouse. These include honoring his wife and providing her with food, clothing, and sexual satisfaction. The traditional *ketubah* also specifies a husband's financial obligations if the marriage ends in divorce.

2. Couples in the Conservative, Reform, and Reconstructionist movements generally choose *ketubot* that express their love for one another rather than one that legally spells out the seemingly male-biased property transfer and conjugal rights which appear in the traditional document. Yet, in the traditional ketubah the husband has obligations to the wife but the wife has none to him.

3. Originally, *ketubot* were written on parchment and often enhanced by drawings and illumination in bright colors.

3. The officiating rabbi or cantor at a wedding will generally provide the couple with a *ketubah*. Often the rabbi will present several choices, including one with traditional language and one which reflects an egalitarian approach to marriage.

4. Often couples prefer to have a personalized *ketubah* designed especially for them by a calligrapher or artist.

5. Here are two sample *ketubot*.

Traditional *Ketubah:*

בְּאֶחָד (בִּשְׁלִישִׁי) בְּשַׁבָּת, אֶחָד עָשָׂר יוֹם (יָמִים)
לַחֹדֶשׁ _____ שְׁנַת חֲמֵשֶׁת אֲלָפִים וְשֵׁשׁ מֵאוֹת
וְ_____ לִבְרִיאַת עוֹלָם לְמִנְיָן שֶׁאָנוּ מוֹנִין כָּאן קָ״ק (עִיר)
מְדִינַת אַמֶּרִיקָה הַצְּפוֹנִית, אֵיךְ הֶחָתָן ר׳_____ בֶּן ר׳
_____ אֲמַר לָהּ לַהֲדָא בְּתוּלְתָּא מָרַת _____ בַּת ר׳
_____, הֲוִי לִי לְאִנְתּוּ כְּדַת מֹשֶׁה וְיִשְׂרָאֵל, וַאֲנָא אֶפְלַח
וְאוֹקִיר אֵיזוֹן וַאֲפַרְנֵס יָתֵיכִי (לִיכִי) כְּהִלְכוֹת גּוּבְרִין יְהוּדָאִין
דְּפָלְחִין וּמוֹקְרִין וְזָנִין וּמְפַרְנְסִין לִנְשֵׁיהוֹן בְּקוּשְׁטָא. וְיָהֵבְנָא לֵיכִי
מֹהַר בְּתוּלַיְכִי כְּסַף זוּזֵי מָאתָן דְּחָזֵי לֵיכִי מִדְּאוֹרַיְתָא, וּמְזוֹנַיְכִי
וּכְסוּתַיְכִי וְסִפּוּקַיְכִי, וּמֵיעַל לְוָתַיְכִי כְּאוֹרַח כָּל אַרְעָא. וּצְבִיאַת
מָרַת _____ בְּתוּלְתָּא דָא וַהֲוַת לֵהּ לְאִנְתּוּ, וְדֵין נְדוּנְיָא
דְּהַנְעֲלַת לֵהּ מִבֵּי אֲבוּהַ בֵּין בְּכֶסֶף בֵּין בִּדְהַב בֵּין בְּתַכְשִׁיטִין,
בְּמָאנֵי דִלְבוּשָׁא, בְּשִׁמּוּשֵׁי דִירָה וּבְשִׁמּוּשֵׁי דְעַרְסָא, הַכֹּל קִבֵּל
עָלָיו ר׳_____ חָתָן דְּנָן בְּמָאָה זְקוּקִים כֶּסֶף צָרוּף. וְצָבִי ר׳
_____ חָתָן דְּנָן וְהוֹסִיף לָהּ מִן דִּילֵהּ עוֹד מֵאָה זְקוּקִים כֶּסֶף
צָרוּף אֲחֵרִים כְּנֶגְדָּן, סַךְ הַכֹּל מָאתַיִם זְקוּקִים כֶּסֶף צָרוּף. וְכָךְ אָמַר
ר׳_____ חָתָן דְּנָן, אַחֲרָיוּת שְׁטַר כְּתוּבְּתָא דָא, נְדוּנְיָא דֵן
וְתוֹסֶפְתָּא דָא קַבֵּלִית עֲלַי וְעַל יָרְתַי בַּתְרַאי לְהִתְפָּרַע מִכָּל שְׁפַר
אֲרַג נִכְסִין וְקִנְיָנִין דְּאִית לִי תְּחוֹת כָּל שְׁמַיָּא, דִּקְנָאִי וּדְעָתִיד אֲנָא
לְמִקְנָא, נִכְסִין דְּאִית לְהוֹן אַחֲרָיוּת וּדְלֵית לְהוֹן אַחֲרָיוּת, כֻּלְּהוֹן
יְהוֹן אַחֲרָאִין וְעַרְבָאִין לִפְרוֹעַ מִנְּהוֹן שְׁטַר כְּתוּבְּתָא דָא, נְדוּנְיָא דֵן
וְתוֹסֶפְתָּא דָא מִנַּאי, וַאֲפִילוּ מִן גְּלִימָא דְעַל כַּתְפַּאי, בְּחַיֵּי וּבָתַר
חַיַּי, מִן יוֹמָא דְּנָן וּלְעָלַם. וְאַחֲרָיוּת שְׁטַר כְּתוּבְּתָא דָא, נְדוּנְיָא דֵן
וְתוֹסֶפְתָּא דָא, קִבֵּל עָלָיו ר׳_____ חָתָן דְּנָן כְּחוֹמֶר כָּל שְׁטָרֵי
כְּתוּבוֹת וְתוֹסֶפְתּוֹת דְּנָהֲגִין בִּבְנוֹת יִשְׂרָאֵל, הָעֲשׂוּיִין כְּתִקּוּן חֲכָמֵינוּ
זִכְרָם לִבְרָכָה, דְּלָא כְּאַסְמַכְתָּא וּדְלָא כְּטוֹפְסֵי דִשְׁטָרֵי. וְקָנִינָא מִן
ר׳_____ בֶּן _____ חָתָן דְּנָן לְמָרַת _____ בַּת
ר׳_____ בְּתוּלְתָּא דָא עַל כָּל מַה דִּכְתוּב וּמְפוֹרָשׁ לְעֵיל
בְּמָאנָא דְּכָשֵׁר לְמִקְנָא בֵּיהּ, וְהַכֹּל שָׁרִיר וְקַיָּם.
נְאוּם _____ בֶּן _____ עֵד.
וּנְאוּם _____ בֶּן _____ עֵד.

On the (first) day of the week, the _____ day of the
month _____ in the year five thousand, six hundred
and _____ since the creation of the world, the era
according to which we are accustomed to reckon here in
the city of (name of city, state, and country), how (name of
bridegroom), son of (name of father), surnamed (family

130

name), said to this virgin (name of bride), daughter of (name of father), surnamed (family name): "Be thou my wife according to the law of Moses and Israel, and I will cherish, honor, support, and maintain thee in accordance with the custom of Jewish husbands who cherish, honor, support, and maintain their wives in truth. And I herewith make for thee the settlement of virgins, two hundred *zuzim,* which belongs to thee, according to the law of Moses and Israel; and I will also give thee thy food, clothing, and necessaries, and live with thee as husband and wife according to universal custom." And Miss (name of bride), this virgin, consented and became his wife. The wedding outfit that she brought unto him from her father's house in silver, gold valuables, wearing apparel, house furniture, and bed clothes, all this (name of bridegroom), the said bridegroom, accepted in the sum of one hundred silver pieces, and (name of bridegroom), the bridegroom, consented to increase this amount from his own property with the sum of one hundred silver pieces, making in all two hundred silver pieces. And thus said (name of bridegroom), the bridegroom: "The responsibility of this marriage contract, of this wedding outfit, and of this additional sum, I take upon myself and my heirs after me, so that they shall be paid from the best part of my property and possession that I have beneath the whole heaven, that which I now possess or may hereafter acquire. All my property, real and personal, even the mantle on my shoulders, shall be mortgaged to secure the payment of this marriage contract, of the wedding outfit, and of the addition made thereto, during my lifetime and after my death, from the present day and forever." (Name of bridegroom), the bridegroom, has taken upon himself the responsibility of this marriage contract, of the wedding outfit and the addition made thereto, according to the restrictive usages of all marriage contracts and the additions thereto made for the daughters of Israel, in accordance with the institution of our sages of blessed memory. It is not to be regarded as a mere forfeiture without consideration or as a mere formula of a document. We have followed the legal formality of symbolical delivery (*kinyan*) between (name of bridegroom), the son of _____, the bridegroom, and (name of bride), the daughter of _____this virgin, and we have used a garment legally fit for the purpose, to strengthen all that is stated above,

And Everything is Valid and Confirmed.

Attested to _____(Witness)

Attested to _____(Witness)

Egalitarian *Ketubah*:

"שבע שמחות את פניך"

בשבת_____ ימים   לחדש _____

שנת_____לבריאת   העולם _____

בעיר _____.

כמנהגי עם ישראל וכדת משה, אנחנו, כן עומדים בנוכחות שפחתנו וחברינן על מנת להיכנס לברית קידושין.

ביום הקידושין שלנו, אנו מקדישים את עצמינו, כרעים אהו־ בים, לעולם ועד בכח תלותנו זה בזו, אנו מתחילים פרשה חדשה זו של חיינו כשווים בצלם אלהים שבנו, שואבים עוז ממעיני האהבה שאיפותינו כרוכים אלו באלו אנו מקדישים את עצמינו להקמת משפחה ובית שיהיו בהם אהבה מסירות לב ליהדות, אנו מאמינים שחיינו ביחד כוונים ביד האלהים הם, ואנו מודים לקדוש ברוך הוא.

וקימנו קנין מן החתן ומן הכלה והכל שריר וקים.

נאום_____עד

נאום_____עד

נאום_____עד

נאום_____עד

"In your presence in perfect joy."

On the _____day of the week, the _____day of the month, in the year _____since the creation of the world corresponding to the _____day of _____nineteen hundred _____in the city of _____, as is the custom of the people of Israel and under the laws of Moses, we _____and _____, stand before our family and friends in order to enter the covenant of marriage.

On this, our wedding day, we consecrate ourselves, as beloved companions, forever. Strengthened by our mutual dependence, we begin our future as equals, empowered by each other's love. Our aspirations are entwined. We devote ourselves to creating a family and home inspired by love and commitment to Judaism. We believe that our life together is *bashert,* [destined by fate] and we are thankful to God.

This contract has been legally acquired and accepted by the groom and the bride. And everything is valid and confirmed.

Attested to _____Witness
Attested to _____Witness
Attested to _____Witness
Attested to _____Witness

Things to remember:

1. Two witnesses are required for the signing of the *ketubah.* This is done prior to the actual wedding ceremony. The witnesses cannot be related by blood or marriage to either the bride or the groom. While Orthodox rabbis and some Conservative rabbis will allow only Jewish men to serve as witnesses, Reform and Reconstructionist rabbis also permit women to serve as witnesses.

2. The *ketubah* is generally signed with complete Hebrew names. Therefore, remind your witnesses to make sure they know their Hebrew names (which include their parents' names). In addition, some *ketubot* include a place for both bride and groom to sign.

3. Part or all of the *ketubah* should be read aloud during the marriage ceremony.

Key words and phrases:

Ayd. עֵד. Witness.
Ketubah כְּתוּבָה (plural *ketubot*). Jewish marriage contract.

If you want to know more:

Ronald H. Isaacs, *The Bride and Groom Handbook* (West Orange, NJ, 1990).
_____, *Rites of Passage: A Guide to the Jewish Life Cycle* (Hoboken, NJ, 1992).
Maurice Lamm, *The Jewish Way in Love and Marriage* (New York, 1980).

Instant Information
Jewish Divorce: The *Get*
גֵּט

The source:

"A man takes a wife and possesses her. She fails to please him . . . and he writes her a bill of divorce" (Deuteronomy 24:1–2). An entire talmudic tractate called *Gittin* (Book of Divorce) is devoted to specific details related to the divorce procedure.

What you need to know:

1. According to Jewish law, a *get* (bill of divorce) is required for every Jewish divorce, whether or not there was a religious marriage ceremony. According to traditional law, the only exception is an interfaith marriage: Jew to non-Jew.

2. Originally, the *get* was a document of twelve lines, written in Hebrew and Aramaic in Torah script on parchment. Today heavy white paper is often used instead of parchment.

3. Each *get* contains the following parts:

   a. A statement that the husband divorces his wife without duress.
   b. A statement that the husband and wife may have no further sexual relationship after the *get* has been written and accepted.
   c. The time and place of the writing of the *get*.
   d. Complete Hebrew names of husband and wife.

4. A *get* is usually written by a *sofer*, a qualified Jewish scribe who has specific expertise in this area. You may want to contact your local rabbi or Jewish Federation for a scribe in your area.

5. The entire procedure may take from one to two hours. The *get* itself is retained by the *Bet Din* (rabbinic court)

and kept in a permanent file. Official letters, called a release or *petur,* are given to the couple after the divorce.

6. In an effort to strive for equal rights in marriage, Reform and Reconstructionist rabbis (and some Conservative rabbis too) will prepare *gittin* which reflect equal participation in a divorce.

7. Here is a sample *get:*

בחמישי בשבת בחמשה ועשרים יום לירח תשרי שנת חמשת
אלפים ושבע מאות ועשרים ושתים לבריאת עולם למנין שאנו
מנין כאן בבאסטאן מתא דיתבא על כיף ימא ועל נהר טשא־
רלעם אנא _____ המכונה _____ בן _____ המ־
כונה _____ העומד היום בבאסטאן מתא דיתבא על כיף
ימא ועל נהר טשארלעס צביתי ברעות נפשי בדלא אניסנא ושב־
קית ופטרית ותרוכית יתיכי ליכי אנת אנתתי _____ המ־
כונה _____ בת _____ דמתקרי _____ ומתקרי
_____ העומדת היום בבאסטאן מתא דיתבא על כיף ימא
ועל נהר טשארלעס דהוית אנתתי מן קדמת דנא וכדו פטרית
ושבקית ותרוכית יתיכי ליכי דיתיהוייין רשאה ושלטאהבנפשיכי
למהך להתנסבא לכל גבר די תיצבייין ואנש לא ימחא בידיכי מן
יומא דנן ולעלם והרי את מותרת לכל אדם ודן די יהוי ליבי מנאי
ספר תרוכין ואגרת שבוקין יגט פטורין כדת משה וישראל

On the _____ day of the week, the _____ day of the month of _____ in the year _____ from the creation of the world according to the calendar reckoning we are accustomed to count here, in the city _____ (which is also known as _____) which is located on the river _____ (and on the river _____) and situated near wells of water, I _____ (also known as _____), the son of _____ (also known as _____), who today am present in the city _____ (which is also known as _____) located on the river _____ (and on the river _____) and situated near wells of water, do willingly consent, being under no restraint, to release, to set free, and put aside you, my wife, _____ (also known as _____), daughter of _____ (also known as _____), which is located on the river _____ (and on the river) and situated near wells of water, who has been my wife from before. Thus I do set free, release you, and put you aside, in order that you may have permission and the authority over yourself to go and marry any man you may desire. No person may hinder you from this day onward, and you are permitted to every man. This shall be for you from me a bill of dismissal, a letter of release, and a document of freedom, in accordance with the laws of Moses and Israel.

_____ the son of _____ Witness

_____ the son of _____ Witness

בחמישי בשבת בחמשה ועשרים יום לירח תשרי שנת חמשת אלפים ושבע מאות ועשרים ושתים

לבריאת עולם למנין שאנו מנין כאן בבאסמאן מתא דיתבא על כיף ימא ועל נהר דיר

טשיארלעס אנא המכונה בן המכונה דיעומד

היום בבאסטאן מתא דיתבא על כיף ימא ועל נהר טשיארלעס צביתי ברעות נפשי

בדלא אניסנא ושיבקית ופטרית ותרוכית יתיכי ליכי אנת אנתתי

העומדת דמתקרי ומתקרי בת המכונה

היום בבאסטאן מתא דיתבא על כיף ימא ועל נהר טשיארלעס דהוית אנתתי מן קדמת

דנא וכדו פטרית ושבקית ותרוכית יתיכי ליכי דידהווייך רשאה ושלטאה בנפשיכי

למהך להתנסבא לכל גבר די תיצבייין ואנש לא ימחא בידיכי מן יומא

דין ולעלם ודהוי ליכי מנאי ספר תרוכין ואגרת שבוקין וגט פטורין

כדת משה וישראל

חיים בן שמעיהו עד

חיים בן נפתלי מרדכי עד

Reprinted with permission from **The Second Jewish Catalogue** by Sharon Strassfeld and Michael Strassfeld © 1976 by the Jewish Publication Society of America.

Things to remember:

1. You will need to have your civil divorce filed before you can obtain a *get*.

2. Sometimes the wife is unable to be present when the *get* is written. In such a case, the husband may appoint an

136

agent (called a *shaliach*) to deliver the *get* to her. If this is not feasible, the husband may authorize his agent to appoint yet another agent to deliver the *get* to his wife. The wife may also appoint an agent to act on her behalf in receiving the *get* from her husband.

3. While some Reform rabbis are more lenient in this regard, all other rabbis require a *get* before performing a marriage for a divorced person.

4. Traditionally, a divorced woman may not marry a *kohen*, a descendant of the priesthood. However, Reform, Reconstructionist, and some Conservative rabbis permit such marriages.

Key words and phrases:

Bet Din בֵּית דִּין. Literally "house of judgment"; a rabbinic court, the witnesses who sign the *get*.

Get גֵט. Jewish divorce.

Ptur פְּטוֹר. Official letter given to husband and wife to certify that their marriage has been dissolved in accordance with Jewish law.

Shaliach שָׁלִיחַ. Agent appointed for to deliver or receive *get* on behalf of husband or wife.

Sofer סוֹפֵר. Scribe.

If you want to know more:

Ronald H. Isaacs, *Rites of Passage: Guide to the Jewish Life Cycle* (Hoboken, NJ, 1992).

Isaac Klein, *A Guide to Jewish Religious Practice* (New York, 1979).

More particulars:

Here is an outline of the process of the presentation of the *get*.

Husband and wife are both asked a number of routine questions to ascertain their free will and consent in the divorce action. For example, the rabbi will begin by asking the husband: "Do you, _____(name of husband), give this *get* of your own free will without duress or compulsion?" After the give-and-take of questions and answers, the rabbi tells the wife to remove all jewelry from her hands, and to hold her hands together with open palms upward in a position to receive the *get*. The scribe folds the *get* and gives it to the rabbi. The rabbi gives the *get* to the husband, who, holding it in both hands, drops it into the palms of the wife and says: "This be your *get*, and with it you are divorced from me from this time forth so that you may become the wife of any man." The wife then receives the *get*, lifts up her hands, walks with the *get* a short distance, and returns. She then gives the *get* to the rabbi, who again reads it with the witnesses. After the proceedings are completed, a tear is made in the *get* to indicate that it has been used and cannot be used again. The document itself is retained by the *Bet Din* in a permanent file. Official letters, called a *ptur* (release), are given to husband and wife to certify that their marriage has been dissolved according to Jewish law.

Instant Information
Hakafot for Simchat Torah
הַקָּפוֹת לְשִׂמְחַת תּוֹרָה

The source:

Seven circuits are mentioned in the Bible. For example, seven circuits were made around Jericho—once a day for six days, and seven times on the seventh day (Joshua 6:14–15). The Mishnah notes that the *lulav* was carried around the Temple altar during the seven days of Sukkot (Sukkah 3:12).

Happy Simchat Torah!!

What you need to know:

1. Today, a single circuit is made around the sanctuary on each of the first six days of the festival of Sukkot (except for the Sabbath) during the chanting of the *hoshannot* (prayers asking God to save us) at the close of the *musaf* additional service. On Hoshannah Rabbah, the seventh day of Sukkot, the procession around the sanctuary with the *lulav* and *etrog* and the Torah scroll is repeated seven times.

2. All but one of the Torah scrolls are carried around the synagogue in processional circuits during both the evening and morning services on the festival of Simchat Torah. Following the circuits, all the worshippers are given an opportunity to be called up to the Torah for an *aliyah*. Unlike other traditional Torah honors, these *aliyot* are intended for a group. Traditionally a *kohen* (priest) is called first, followed by a Levite and then by ordinary Israelites. Finally come the persons honored with the last *aliyah* in Deuteronomy and the first in Genesis, who stand under a *tallit* (prayer shawl) held up by those on the perimeter. The last *aliyah* is reserved for children.

3. Hasidim also perform these circuits at the conclusion of the evening service on Shemini Atzeret; in Reform congregations they are also performed on Shemini

Atzeret. However, since the Reform movement does not acknowledge the distinction between Israelites, priests, and Levites, different assignments are made.

4. There are texts that are read aloud to accompany each circuit on Simchat Torah. After each one it is customary to dance with and around the Torah scrolls, singing appropriate songs.

Read:

אָנָּא יהוה הוֹשִׁיעָה נָּא, אָנָּא יהוה הַצְלִיחָה נָא, אָנָּא יהוה
עֲנֵנוּ בְיוֹם קָרְאֵנוּ:

O God, we beseech You, save us, and cause us to prosper. O God, answer us when we call. *Aneinu v'yom koreinu.*

Read:

אֱלֹהֵי הָרוּחוֹת הוֹשִׁיעָה נָּא, בּוֹחֵן לְבָבוֹת הַצְלִיחָה נָא, גּוֹאֵל
חָזָק עֲנֵנוּ בְיוֹם קָרְאֵנוּ:

God of all spirits, save us. Searcher of our hearts, cause us to prosper. Mighty Redeemer, answer us when we call. *Aneinu v'yom koreinu.*

Now march in the first *hakafah.*

Read:

דּוֹבֵר צְדָקוֹת הוֹשִׁיעָה נָּא, הָדוּר בִּלְבוּשׁוֹ הַצְלִיחָה נָא, וָתִיק
וְחָסִיד עֲנֵנוּ בְיוֹם קָרְאֵנוּ:

Dispenser of righteousness, save us. God clothed in splendor, cause us to prosper. With everlasting love, answer us when we call. *Aneinu v'yom koreinu.*

Now march in the second *hakafah.*

Read:

זַךְ וְיָשָׁר הוֹשִׁיעָה נָּא, חוֹמֵל דַּלִּים הַצְלִיחָה נָא, טוֹב וּמֵטִיב
עֲנֵנוּ בְיוֹם קָרְאֵנוּ:

Pure and Upright One, save us. You who are gracious to the needy, cause us to prosper. Good and benevolent God, answer us when we call. *Aneinu v'yom koreinu.*

Now march in the third *hakafah*.

Read:

יוֹדֵעַ מַחֲשָׁבוֹת הוֹשִׁיעָה נָּא, כַּבִּיר וְנָאוֹר הַצְלִיחָה נָא, לוֹבֵשׁ צְדָקוֹת עֲנֵנוּ בְיוֹם קָרְאֵנוּ:

You who know our thoughts, save us. Mighty One, cause us to prosper. God robed in righteousness, answer us when we call. *Aneinu v'yom koreinu.*

Now march in the fourth *hakafah*.

Read:

מֶלֶךְ עוֹלָמִים הוֹשִׁיעָה נָּא, נָאוֹר וְאַדִּיר הַצְלִיחָה נָא, סוֹמֵךְ נוֹפְלִים עֲנֵנוּ בְיוֹם קָרְאֵנוּ:

Eternal Ruler, save us. Source of light and majesty, cause us to prosper. Upholder of the fallen, answer us when we call. *Aneinu v'yom koreinu.*

Now march in the fifth *hakafah*.

Read:

עוֹזֵר דַּלִים הוֹשִׁיעָה נָּא, פּוֹדֶה וּמַצִּיל הַצְלִיחָה נָא, צוּר עוֹלָמִים עֲנֵנוּ בְיוֹם קָרְאֵנוּ:

Helper of those in need, save us. Redeemer and Deliverer, cause us to prosper. Everlasting Rock, answer us when we call. *Aneinu v'yom koreinu.*

Now march in the sixth *hakafah*.

Read:

קָדוֹשׁ וְנוֹרָא הוֹשִׁיעָה נָּא, רַחוּם וְחַנּוּן הַצְלִיחָה נָא, שׁוֹמֵר הַבְּרִית עֲנֵנוּ בְיוֹם קָרְאֵנוּ:

Holy, Awesome One, save us. Compassionate One, cause us to prosper. Perfect in all ways, answer us when we call. *Aneinu v'yom koreinu.*

Read:

תּוֹמֵךְ תְּמִימִים הוֹשִׁיעָה נָּא, תַּקִּיף לָעַד הַצְלִיחָה נָא, תָּמִים בְּמַעֲשָׂיו עֲנֵנוּ בְיוֹם קָרְאֵנוּ:

141

Upholder of the innocent, save us. Eternal in power, cause us to prosper. Perfect in Your ways, answer us when we call. *Aneinu v'yom koreinu.*

Now march in the seventh *hakafah.*

Things to remember:

1. Many congregations provide flags to be carried during the *hakafot* processionals on Simchat Torah. You may want to make your own original banner in advance and bring it to services.

2. There are other kinds of processionals besides those during Simchat Torah (and regular Torah readings). At a traditional wedding, for example, the bride circles the groom (three or seven times, depending on the tradition of the community). In Sephardic and Hasidic communities, individuals walk around a coffin seven times prior to the burial. Some people also follow the custom of making a processional around the cemetery when praying for the sick. In addition, Torah scrolls are carried around in a processional circuit during the dedication ceremonies of synagogues and cemeteries.

3. Children often parade with miniature (toy) Torah scrolls.

Key words and phrases:

Aneinu v'yom koreinu עֲנֵנוּ בְיוֹם קָרְאֵנוּ. Answer us when we call.

Hakafah הַקָפָה (plural, *hakafot* הַקָפוֹת). Ceremonial processional circuits with Torah scrolls around the synagogue.

Hoshanah הוֹשַׁעְנָה (plural *hoshanot* הוֹשַׁעְנוֹת). Verses asking God to save us.

If you want to know more:

Philip Birnbaum, *A Book of Jewish Concepts* (New York, 1964).

Encyclopaedia Judaica (Jerusalem, 1971), 7:1154.

Ronald H. Isaacs and Kerry M. Olitzky, *Sacred Celebrations: A Jewish Holiday Handbook* (Hoboken, NJ, 1994).

More particulars:

Some people leave the synagogue and do their *hakafot* for Simchat Torah around the outside of the building or parade in the neighborhood.

Instant Information
Who's Who and What's What on a Page of . . . ?
דַּף

The source:

The first five books of the Bible, also known as the Five Books of Moses and as the Pentateuch, are collectively called the *Chumash* and are also often referred to as the Torah; the entire Hebrew Bible is known as the *Tanach.* The Talmud is referred to as the Oral Torah, in contradistinction to the biblical text, which is known as the Written Torah. According to tradition, both Torahs were given by God to Moses on Mount Sinai. Moses immediately wrote down the Written Torah, but it took a long time before the Oral Torah was written down in the form of the two Talmuds, one in Eretz Israel (often referred to as the Palestinian Talmud) and the other in Babylonia (the Babylonian Talmud).

What you need to know:

1. This is what you will find on a page of Torah text in the *Mikra'ot Gedolot,* a classic arrangement of commentaries on the Hebrew Bible.

> a. *Targum.* Aramaic translation of the Torah attributed to Onkelos (2nd cent. C.E.) and therefore referred to as Targum Onkelos. Since all translation is interpretation, this is an important tool for understanding the text. It gives us an idea of how the Hebrew text was understood nearly two thousand years ago and is especially useful in regard to unusual words and ancient customs or practices.
> b. *Rashi's Commentary.* By Rabbi Shlomo Yitzchaki (France, 1040–1105); particularly important because

of Rashi's encyclopedic grasp of the entire Jewish tradition.

c. *Ibn Ezra's Commentary.* By Avraham ben Meir Ibn Ezra (Spain, 1093–1167); stresses grammar and other literary matters.

d. *Supercommentary on Ibn Ezra.* By Rabbi Shlomo Zalman Netter (Austria-Hungary, 19th century): explains difficult points in Ibn Ezra's commentary.

e. *Sforno's Commentary.* By Ovadia Sforno (Italy, 1475–1550); literal explanation of text.

f. *Rashbam's Commentary.* By Shmuel ben Meir (France, 1080–1174), the grandson of Rashi; explicates simple meaning of text.

g. *Masorah.* Notes and rules concerning writing, spacing, paragraphing, and correct vowelization of text (which originally was written without vowels), prepared by Masoretes in Tiberias (6th–10th cent.).

h. *Toldot Aharon.* Cross-references to talmudic passages where biblical text under discussion is cited.

2. This is what you will find on a page of Talmud text:

a. *Mishnah.* Text of Oral Law.

b. *Gemara.* Rabbinic discussions of Mishnah, redacted around 500 C.E.

c. *Rashi.* Commentary on Talmud by Rabbi Shlomo Yitzchaki (France, 1040–1105).

d. *Tosafot.* Collected comments of Rashi's descendants, his disciples and the schools they founded.

e. *Ein Mishpat.* Cross-references to code of Maimonides (*Mishneh Torah*) and other legal collections.

f. *Commentary of Rav Nissim Gaon.* References of quotations encountered in the course of Talmudic study, as well as source and parallels (North Africa, 11th cent.).

g. *Gilyon Hashas.* Textual notes by Rabbi Akiva Eger (Germany, 1761–1837).

h. *Hagahot Ha'bach.* Marginal notes by Rabbi Yoel Sirkes (Poland, 1561–1640).

i. *Mesoret Ha'shas.* Cross-references to other volumes of Talmud.

Things to remember:

1. Traditional writings on the Torah fall into two categories, *midrash halachah* (legal material) and *midrash aggadah* (nonlegal material).

2. The Babylonian Talmud is paginated according to the front (a) and back (b) side of each page; thus, for example, the sequence would be 1a, 1b, 2a, 2b, and so forth.

3. The Mishnah and Gemara together make up the Talmud. The Gemara includes legal discussions as well as historical records, legends, parables, and ethical discussions.

Key words and phrases:

Masorah מְסוֹרָה. Jewish tradition in general; more specifically, rules regarding the traditional text of the Hebrew Bible.

Midrash aggadah מִדְרָשׁ אַגָּדָה. Nonlegal material, as found, for instance, in Midrash Rabbah, Tanhuma, and Pesikta deRab Kahana.

Midrash halachah מִדְרָשׁ הֲלָכָה. Legal material, including Mishnah and Gemara (i.e., the two Talmuds), early (Geonic) responsa, codes (including those by Alfasi, and Rashi as well as the *Mishneh Torah, Tur,* and *Shulchan Aruch*), and later rabbinic responsa.

Mikra'ot Gedolot מִקְרָאוֹת גְדוֹלוֹת. Often called Rabbinic Bible; contains various commentaries.

Mishnah מִשְׁנָה. From the word שָׁנָה meaning "to repeat"; codification of Oral Law prepared by Rabbi Judah Hanasi in 200 C.E., divided into six parts, and subdivided into sixty-three tractates.

Rashbam רַשְׁבַּ"ם. Rabbi Shmuel ben Meir, Rashi's grandson; author of commentary that supplements Rashi's.

Rashi רַשִׁ"י. Rabbi Solomon ben Isaac or Shlomo Yitzchaki, the classic Jewish commentator on both Bible and Talmud.

Supercommentary. Commentary on some other commentary.

If you want to know more:

Joel Lurie Grishaver, *Learning Torah: A Self-Guided Journey Through the Layers of Jewish Learning* (New York, 1990).

A Page from . . . the Torah, Talmud, Midrash, Mishneh Torah, Shulchan Aruch (New York, n.d.).

More particulars:

In the modern sense of the word, one might "study" the Bible by reading its text from beginning to end and thinking about it. In the traditional sense, however, one reads the Torah in uniform increments rather than all at once (the weekly portions read aloud in the synagogue each Sabbath) and gleans an understanding of the text by means of the commentaries found in a source like *Mikra'ot Gedolot*.

Instant Information
Jewish Acronyms
רָאשֵׁי תֵּיבוֹת

The source:

Acronyms are abbreviations derived from the initial letters of combinations of words. They are shortcut for long names and terms. The Jewish cultural universe is replete with acronyms of many kinds. Some, like the word *Tanach,* date back to the talmudic period.

What you need to know:

Rabbinic Acronyms

Besht	Rabbi Israel Baal Shem Tov
HaGra	Rabbi Elijah ben Solomon Zalman (the Vilna Gaon)
Ralbag	Rabbi Levi ben Gerson (Gersonides)
Ramaz	Rabbi Moses Zacuto
Rambam	Rabbi Moses ben Maimon (Maimonides)
Ramban	Rabbi Moses ben Nachman (Nachmanides)
Rashbam	Rabbi Samuel ben Meir
Rashi	Rabbi Solomon bar Isaac
Rif	Rabbi Isaac ben Jacob Alfasi

Religious Organizations

Reform

AAC	American Conference of Cantors
ARZA	Association of Reform Zionists of America
CCAR	Central Conference of American Rabbis
HUC-JIR	Hebrew Union College–Jewish Institute of Religion
NATA	National Association of Temple Administrators

148

NATE	National Association of Temple Educators
NFTY	North American Federation of Temple Youth
UAHC	Union of American Hebrew Congregations
WRJ	Women of Reform Judaism (formerly, National Federation of Temple Sisterhoods)

Conservative

CA	Cantors' Assembly
EA	Educators' Assembly
JTS	Jewish Theological Seminary of America
RA	Rabbinical Assembly
UJ	University of Judaism
USCJ	United Synagogue of Conservative Judaism (formerly United Synagogue of America)
USY	United Synagogue Youth
UTCJ	Union of Traditional Conservative Judaism

Orthodox

CAA	Cantorial Association of America
RAA	Rabbinical Association of America
RCA	Rabbinical Council of America
UOJCA	Union of Orthodox Jewish Congregations of America (also known as the OU)
UOR	Union of Orthodox Rabbis
YU	Yeshiva University

Reconstructionist

FRSH	Federation of Reconstructionist Synagogues and Havurot
JRF	Jewish Reconstructionist Foundation
RRA	Reconstructionist Rabbinical Association
RRC	Reconstructionist Rabbinical College

Zionist Organizations

ARZA	Association of Reform Zionists of America
AZF	American Zionist Federation
AZYF	American Zionist Youth Foundation
JNF	Jewish National Fund
LZA	Labor Zionist Organization
MERCAZ	Movement to Reaffirm Conservative Zionism
ZOA	Zionist Organization of America

Youth Organizations

BBYO	B'nai B'rith Youth Organization
NCSY	National Council of Synagogue Youth
NFTY	North American Federation of Temple Youth
USY	United Synagogue Youth

Defense Organizations

ADL	Anti-Defamation League of B'nai B'rith
AJC	American Jewish Committee
AJC	American Jewish Congress
JDL	Jewish Defense League

Books

AJYB	*American Jewish Year Book*
EJ	*Encyclopaedia Judaica*
JE	*Jewish Encyclopaedia*
Tanach	The Hebrew Bible, comprising *Torah, Nevi'im* (Prophets), and *Ketuvim* (Writings)
UJE	*Universal Jewish Encyclopedia*

Charitable Organizations

AJC	Allied Jewish Charities
CJA	Combined Jewish Appeal
CJF	Council of Jewish Federations
CJP	Council of Jewish Philanthropies
FJC	Federated Jewish Charities

FJP	Federation of Jewish Philanthropies
HIAS	Hebrew Immigrant Aid Society
JFA	Jewish Federated Appeal
UHC	United Hebrew Charities
UJA	United Jewish Appeal

Other Organizations

AAAPME	American Academic Association for Peace in the Middle East
AIPAC	American Israel Public Affairs Committee
AJCW	Association of Jewish Center Workers
AJHS	American Jewish Historical Society
CAJE	Coalition for the Advancement of Jewish Education
GA	General Assembly (annual meeting of Jewish federations)
JDC	Joint Distribution Committee
JESNA	Jewish Education Service of North America
JTA	Jewish Telegraphic Agency
JWV	Jewish War Veterans
NCJW	National Council of Jewish Women
NCSJ	National Conference on Soviet Jewry
NJCRAC	National Jewish Community Relations Advisory Council
SCA	Synagogue Council of America
SSSJ	Student Struggle for Soviet Jewry
WJC	World Jewish Congress
WUJS	World Union of Jewish Students

Key words and phrases:

Rashei tevot רָאשֵׁי תֵּיבוֹת. Abbreviation or acronym.

If you want to know more:

Ronald H. Isaacs, *The Jewish Information Source Book* (Northvale, NJ, 1993).

Richard Siegel and Carl Rheins, eds., *The Jewish Almanac* (New York, 1980).

Instant Information
Jewish Surnames and Their Meanings
שֵׁם הַמִּשְׁפָּחָה

The source:

In ancient and medieval times Jews did not have surnames and were generally known only by their given name and patronymic (father's name), in the form X ben (son of) Y. When Jewish families began adopting surnames in the modern era, they took them from a plethora of sources, including occupations, physical characteristics, nicknames, and geographical locations. Often, surnames were assigned to individuals by government officials.

What you need to know:

The following is a sample of European Jewish surnames and their meanings:

Occupational Names

Abzug: printer
Ackerman: plowman
Alembik: distiller
Antman: handyman
Becker: baker
Berger: shepherd
Bernstein: amber dealer
Braverman: brewer
Bronfman: whiskey dealer
Bulka: baker
Burla: jeweler
Chait: tailor
Chazin: cantor
Citron: lemon seller
Drucker: printer
Einstein: mason

Feder: scribe
Flaxman: flax merchant
Fleischer: butcher
Galinsky: grain merchant
Geiger: violinist
Glass: glass trade
Imber: ginger seller
Kadar: cooper
Klinger: junk dealer
Kolatch: baker
Kushner: furrier
Marmelstein: builder
Messinger: brass dealer
Pechenik: baker
Perlmutter: pearl dealer
Plotkin: fish dealer

Portnoy: tailor
Scharfstein: knife grinder
Schloss: lock maker
Singer: cantor

Tabachnik: snuff maker
Wapner: lime dealer
Weberl: weaver

Physical Characteristics

Album: white
Blau: blonde
Bleich: pale
Dick: stout
Geller: yellow
Gross: large
Jung: young

Klein: small
Kraus: curly
Kurtz: short
Roth: red
Schwartz: black
Stark: strong
Weiss: white

Geographical Names

Altfeld: Poland
Apter: Galicia
Auerbach: Germany
Barr: Ukraine
Bolotin: Poland
Burnstein: Poland
Chomsky: White Russia
Eisenberg: Hungary
Floss: Bavaria
Fuld: Germany
Ginsburg: Bavaria
Halperin: Germany

Jastrow: Prussia
Kissinger: Germany
Kutner: Poland
Lapin: Poland
Lubin: Poland
Mintz: Germany
Pilch: Poland
Sturm: Poland
Teplitz: Czechoslovakia
Warburg: Germany
Yampol: Russia

Names Derived from Religious Status

Kohen	*Levi*
Cohen	Levi
Kogan	Levy
Cogan	Levin
Cohn	Levine
Kahn	Levinsky
Kaplan	Levitt
Katz	Levinthal

If you want to know more:

Heinrich and Eva Guggenheimer, *Jewish Family Names and Their Origins: An Etymological Dictionary* (Hoboken, NJ, 1992).

Benzion C. Kaganoff, *A Dictionary of Jewish Names and Their History* (New York, 1977).

The source:

Rabbi Solomon Yitzchaki (1040–1105), known by the acronym Rashi, was medieval Jewry's foremost commentator on the Bible and Talmud. When the first Hebrew Bibles were printed in the sixteenth century, his commentary was included, but in a distinctive typeface that set it off from the biblical text on the same page. Because of its association with Rashi, the new typeface soon came to be known as "Rashi script." Almost all of the commentaries on the Talmud and Bible are still printed in Rashi script. In fact, the ability to read Rashi script is an essential skill for studying this literature.

What you need to know:

Here is the Hebrew alphabet in Rashi script.

ﬡ ﬢ ﬖ ﬔ ﬓ ﬕ ﬗ ﬘ ﬙ ﬚ ﬛ ﬠ ﬡ ﬢ ﬣ ﬤ ﬥ ﬦ ﬧ ﬨ ﬩

Key words and phrases:

K'tav Rashi כְּתַב רַשִׁי. Rashi script.

Things to remember:

1. There are other commentaries besides those attributed to Rashi that are written in Rashi script.

2. Rashi's commentary is important because it is encyclopedic in nature (and pre-CD ROM).

If you want to know more:

Encyclopaedia Judaica (London, 1973), 13:1558–65.

Instant Information
Who's Who in the Bible
תַּנַ"ך

What you need to know:

The following is an alphabetical list of important person-
alities in the Torah, the Five Books of Moses:

Aaron: Elder brother of Moses.
Abel: Second son of Adam and Eve.
Abraham: First patriarch and founder of Hebrew
   nation.
Adam and Eve: First man and woman in the Bible.
Balaam: Heathen prophet whose intended curse of
   the Israelites turned into a blessing.
Balak: King of Moab.
Benjamin: Youngest son of Jacob.
Cain: Eldest son of Adam and Eve.
Caleb: Leader of tribe of Judah.
Dan: Fifth son of Jacob.
Dinah: Daughter of Jacob and Leah.
Enoch: Eldest son of Cain.
Ephraim: Youngest son of Joseph.
Esau: Son of Isaac and elder twin brother of Jacob.
Gad: Seventh son of Jacob.
Gershon: Eldest of Levi's three sons.
Hagar: Mother of Ishmael and Egyptian handmaid of
   Sarah.
Ham: Son of Noah.
Haran: Brother of Abraham.
Heth: Son of Canaan.
Isaac: Second of the three patriarchs.
Ishmael: Eldest son of Abraham.
Israel: New name given to Jacob.
Issachar: Fifth son of Jacob and Leah.
Jacob: Third of the patriarchs.
Japheth: Son of Noah.
Jethro: Midianite priest and father of Zipporah.

Joseph: Son of Jacob and Rachel.

Judah: Fourth son of Jacob's first wife, Leah.

Keturah: Abraham's second wife.

Korah: Levite related to Moses who rebelled against Moses and Aaron.

Laban: Brother of Rebeccah.

Lamech: Father of Noah.

Leah: Daughter of Laban and wife of Jacob.

Levi: Third son of Jacob and Leah.

Lot: Son of Abraham's brother Haran.

Manasseh: First son of Joseph and Asenath.

Melchizedek: King of Salem.

Methusaleh: Son of Enoch and oldest person recorded in the Bible.

Miriam: Elder sister of Moses.

Moses: Prophet and founder of Jewish people.

Nahshon: Chief of tribe of Judah.

Naphtali: Sixth son of Jacob.

Noah: Hero of the flood narratives.

Onan: Son of Judah.

Pharaoh: Permanent title of king of Egypt in ancient times.

Phineas. Priest and grandson of Aaron.

Potiphar: Chief of Pharaoh's bodyguard.

Puah: One of midwives who disobeyed Pharaoh's orders to kill the Hebrew male children at birth.

Rachel: Second wife of Jacob.

Rebeccah: Wife of Isaac and mother of Jacob and Esau.

Reuben: Eldest son of Jacob and Leah.

Sarah: Wife of Abraham and mother of Isaac.

Shem: Son of Noah.

Simeon: Second son of Jacob.

Tamar: Wife of Er.

Terah: Father of Abraham.

Zebulun: Sixth son of Jacob and Leah.

Zelophehad: Israelite of the tribe of Manasseh whose five daughters claimed the right, until then reserved to sons, to inherit their father's land.

Zipporah: Wife of Moses.

Judges

The period of the judges, or civic leaders of the community, began with the death of Joshua and ended during the lifetime of the prophet Samuel. This is a list of the judges, as they appear in the Bible:

Othniel
Ehud
Shamgar
Barak
Gideon
Abimelech
Tola
Jair

Jephthah
Ibzan
Elon
Abdon
Samson
Eli, the priest
Samuel the prophet

Kings of Israel

After the period of judges, Israel was ruled by kings. Their names are listed below.

United Kingdom	Kingdom of Judah	Kingdom of Israel
Saul	Rehoboam	Jeroboam I
David	Abijah	Nadab
Solomon	Asa	Baasha
Judah	Jehoshaphat	Elah
	Jehoram	Zimri
	Ahaziah	Omri
	Athaliah	Ahab
	Jehoash	Ahaziah
	Amaziah	Jehoram
	Uzziah	Jehu
	Jotham	Jehoahaz
	Ahaz	Jehoash
	Hezekiah	Jeroboam II
	Manasseh	Zechariah
	Amon	Shallum
	Josiah	Menahem
	Jehoahaz	Pekahiah
	Jehoiakim	Pekah
	Jehoiachin	Hoshea
	Zedekiah	Joash

Prophets

Prophets acted as spokespersons for God. They often arose at times of political or social crisis. Here is a list of the forty- eight persons granted the gift of prophecy in the period after the conquest of Canaan. Those whose prophetic utterances were set down in writing and included in the Bible are indicated by an asterisk.

Joshua
Phinehas
Elkanah
David
Samuel
Asir
Elkanah, son of Korah
Abiasaph
Gad
Nathan
Asaph
Heman
Ethan
Jeduthun
Ahijah
Shemaiah
Iddo
Azariah
Hanani
Jehu
Micaiah
Eleazar
Elijah
Elisha

Jonah*
Obadiah*
Zechariah
Amoz
Oded
Hosea*
Amos*
Isaiah*
Micah*
Joel*
Nahum*
Habakkuk*
Zephaniah*
Jeremiah*
Uriah
Ezekiel*
Baruch
Seraiah
Daniel
Mordecai
Haggai*
Zechariah*
Malachi*

The seven female prophets were:

Sarah
Miriam
Deborah
Hannah

Abigail
Huldah
Esther

If you want to know more:

Joan Comay, *Who's Who in the Old Testament* (Nashville, 1971).

Kerry M. Olitzky and Ronald H. Isaacs, *A Glossary of Jewish Life* (Northvale, NJ, 1992).

P. Wollman Tsamir, *Graphic History of the Jewish Heritage* (New York, 1963).

More particulars:

In the preceding lists, we have used the conventional English spellings of the names from the Bible. They may differ somewhat from the spellings you will find elsewhere, especially when transliterated directly from the Hebrew.

Instant Information
The 613 Commandments
תַּרְיַ"ג מִצְוֹת

The source:

The total number of biblical commandments (both precepts and prohibitions) is given in rabbinic tradition as 613. Rabbi Simlai, one of the talmudic sages, stated: "613 commandments were revealed to Moses at Sinai, 365 prohibitions equal in number to the solar days, and 248 mandates corresponding to the number of limbs of the human body" (Babylonian Talmud, Makkot 23b).

What you need to know:

The following is a summary of the 613 commandments as prepared by Moses Maimonides in his *Book of Commandments.* His version is accepted by the majority of teachers and scholars.

Positive Commandments

The Jew is required to (1) believe that God exists and (2) acknowledge God's unity; to (3) love, (4) fear, and (5) serve God. The Jew is also instructed to (6) cleave to God (by associating with and imitating the wise) and to (7) swear only by God's name. One must (8) imitate God and (9) sanctify God's name.

The Jew must (10) recite the *Shema* each morning and evening and (11) study the Torah and teach it to others. The Jew must bind *tefillin* on (12) head and (13) arm. The Jew must make (14) *tzitzit* for the garments and (15) fix a *mezuzah* on the door. The people are to be (16) assembled every seventh year to hear the Torah read, and (17) the king must write a special copy of the Torah for himself. (18) Every Jew is to have a Torah scroll. One must (19) praise God after eating.

The Jews are to (20) build a Temple and (21) respect it. It must be (22) guarded at all times, and (23) the Levites are to perform their special duties in it. Before entering the Temple or participating in its service, the priests (24) must wash their hands and feet; they must also (25) light the candelabrum daily. The priests are required to (26) bless Israel and (27) set the shewbread and frankincense before the Ark. Twice daily they must (28) burn the incense on the golden altar. (29) Fire shall be kept burning on the altar continually, and the ashes must be (30) removed daily. Ritually unclean persons must be (31) kept out of the Temple. Israel (32) is to honor its priests, who must be (33) dressed in special priestly raiment. The priests are to (34) carry the Ark on their shoulders, and (35) the holy anointing oil must be prepared according to its special formula. (36) The priestly families are to officiate in rotation. In honor of certain dead close relative the priests must (37) make themselves ritually unclean. The high priest may marry (38) only a virgin.

The (39) *tamid* sacrifice must be offered twice daily, and the (40) high priest must also offer a meal-offering twice daily. An additional sacrifice (*musaf*) must be offered (41) every Sabbath, (42) on the first of every month, and (43) on each of the seven days of Passover. On the second day of Passover (44) a meal offering of the first barley must also be brought. On Shavuot a (45) *musaf* must be offered and (46) two loaves of bread as a wave-offering. The additional sacrifice must also be made on (47) Rosh Hashanah and (48) on the Day of Atonement when the (49) *Avodah* must also be performed. On every day of the festival of (50) Sukkot a *musaf* must be brought, as well as on the (51) eighth day thereof.

Every male [and female] Jew is to make (52) pilgrimage to the Temple three times a year and (53) appear there during the three pilgrim festivals. One must (54) rejoice on the festivals.

On the fourteenth of Nisan one must (55) slaughter the paschal lamb, and one must (56) eat of its roasted flesh on the night of the fifteenth. Those who were ritually impure in Nisan are to slaughter the paschal lamb on the (57) fourteenth of Iyar and eat it with (58) *matzah* and bitter herbs. Trumpets should be (59) sounded when the festive sacrifices are brought and also in times of tribulation.

Cattle to be sacrificed must be (60) at least eight days old and (61) without blemish. All offerings must be (62) salted. It is a *mitzvah* to perform the ritual of (63) the burnt-offering, (64) the sin-offering, (65) the guilt-offering, (66) the peace-offering, and (67) the meal-offering.

Should the Sanhedrin err in a decision, its members (68) must bring a sin-offering, which offering must also be brought (69) by a person who has unwittingly transgressed a *karet* prohibition [i.e., an act which incurs *karet* if done deliberately]. When in doubt as to whether one has transgressed such a prohibition, a (70) "suspensive" guilt-offering must be brought.

For (71) stealing or swearing falsely and for other sins of a like nature, a guilt-offering must be brought. In special circumstances the sin-offering (72) can be according to one's means.

One must (73) confess one's sins before God and repent for them.

A (74) man or (75) woman who has a seminal issue must bring sacrifice; a woman must also bring a sacrifice (76) after childbirth.

A leper must (77) bring a sacrifice after he [or she] has been cleansed.

One must (78) tithe one's cattle. The (79) firstborn of clean [i.e., permitted] cattle are holy and must be sacrificed. Firstborn sons must be (80) redeemed. The firstling of the ass must be (81) redeemed; if not (82) its neck has to be broken.

Animals set aside as offerings (83) must be brought to Jerusalem without delay and (84) may be sacrificed only in the Temple. Offerings from outside the land of Israel (85) may also be brought to the Temple.

Sanctified animals (86) which have become blemished must be redeemed. A beast exchanged for an offering (87) is also holy.

The priests must eat (88) the remainder of the meal-offering and (89) the flesh of sin- and guilt-offerings; but consecrated flesh which has become (90) ritually unclean or (91) which was not eaten within its appointed time must be burned.

A Nazirite must (92) let his hair grow during the period of his separation. When that period is over he must (93) shave his head and bring his sacrifice.

A person must (94) honor his vows and oaths which a judge can (95) annul only in accordance with the law.

162

Anyone who touches (96) a carcass or (97) one of the eight species of reptiles becomes ritually unclean; food becomes unclean by (98) coming into contact with a ritually unclean object. Menstruous women (99) and those lying-in after childbirth (100) are ritually impure. A leper (101), a leprous garment (102), and a leprous house (103) are all ritually unclean. A man having a (104) running issue is unclean, as is (105) semen. A woman suffering from (106) a running issue is also impure. A human corpse (107) is ritually unclean. The purification water (*mei niddah*) purifies (108) the unclean, but makes the clean ritually impure. It is a *mitzvah* to become ritually clean (109) by ritual immersion. To become cleansed of leprosy one (110) one must follow the specified procedure and also (111) shave off all of one's hair. Until cleansed the leper (112) must be bareheaded with clothing in disarray so as to be easily distinguishable.

The ashes of (113) the red heifer are to be used in the process of ritual purification.

If a person (114) undertakes to give his [or her] own value to the Temple, he [or she] must do so. Should a person declare an unclean beast (115), a house (116), or a field (117) as a donation to the Temple, he must give their value in money as fixed by the priest. If one unwittingly derives benefit from Temple property (118), full restitution plus a fifth must be made.

The fruit of (119) the fourth year's growth of trees is holy and may be eaten only in Jerusalem. When you reap your fields you must leave the corners (120), the gleanings (121), the forgotten sheaves (122), the misformed bunches of grapes (123), and the gleanings of the grapes (124) for the poor.

The first fruits must be (125) separated and brought to the Temple, and you must also (126) separate the great heave-offering (*terumah*) and give it to the priests. You must give (127) one tithe of your produce to the Levites and separate (128) a second tithe which is to be eaten only in Jerusalem. The Levites (129) must give a tenth of their tithe to the priests.

In the third and sixth years of the seven-year cycle you must (130) separate a tithe for the poor instead of a second tithe. A declaration (131) must be recited when separating the various tithes and (132) when bringing the first fruits to the Temple. The first portion of the (133) dough must be given to the priest.

In the seventh year (*shemittah*) everything that grows is (134) ownerless and available to all; the fields (135) must lie fallow and you may not till the ground. You must (136) sanctify the Jubilee [fiftieth] year, and on the Day of Atonement in that year (137) you must sound the *shofar* and set all Hebrew slaves free. In the Jubilee year all land is to be (138) returned to its ancestral owners; and generally, in a walled city (139) the seller has the right to buy back a house within a year of the sale.

Starting from entry into the land of Israel, the years of the Jubilee must be (140) counted and announced yearly and septennially.

In the seventh year (141) all debts are annulled, but (142) one may exact a debt owed by a foreigner.

When you slaughter an animal you must (143) give the priest his share just as you must also give him (144) the first of the fleece. When a person makes a *cherem* [special vow], you must (145) distinguish between what belongs to the Temple [i.e., when God's name is mentioned in the vow] and between what goes to the priests. To be fit for consumption, beast and fowl must be (146) slaughtered according to the law, and if they are not of a domesticated species (147) their blood must be covered with earth after the slaughtering.

Set the parent bird (148) free when taking the nest. Examine beast (149), fowl (150), locusts (151), and fish (152) to determine whether they are permitted for consumption.

The Sanhedrin is to (153) sanctify the first day of every month and reckon the years and the seasons.

You must (154) rest on the Sabbath day and (155) declare it holy at its onset and termination. On the fourteenth of Nisan (156) remove all leaven from your ownership, and on the night of the fifteenth (157) relate the story of the Exodus from Egypt; on that night (158) you must also eat *matzah*. On the (159) first and (160) seventh days of Passover you must rest. Starting from the first day of the first sheaf [the sixteenth of Nisan] you shall (161) count forty-nine days. You must rest on (162) Shavuot and on (163) Rosh Hashanah; on the Day of Atonement you must (164) fast and (165) rest. You must also rest on (166) the first and

(167) the eighth day of Sukkot, during which festival you shall (168) dwell in booths and (169) take the four species. On Rosh Hashanah (170) you are to hear the sound of the *shofar*.

Every male is to (171) give half a shekel to the Temple annually. You must (172) obey a prophet and (173) appoint a king. You must also (174) obey the Sanhedrin; in the case of a division, (175) yield to the majority. Judges and officials shall be (176) appointed in every town and they shall judge the people (177) impartially.

Whoever is aware of evidence (178) must come to court to testify. Witnesses shall be (179) examined thoroughly and, if found to be false, (180) shall have done to them what they intended to do to the accused.

When a person is found murdered and the murderer is unknown, the ritual of (181) decapitating the heifer must be performed.

Six cities of refuge are to be (182) established. The Levites, who have no ancestral share in the land, shall (183) be given cities to live in.

You must (184) build a fence around your roof and remove potential hazards from your home.

Idolatry and its appurtenances (185) must be destroyed, and a city which has become perverted must be (186) treated according to the law. You are instructed to (187) destroy the seven Canaanite nations, and (188) blot out the memory of Amalek, and (189) to remember what they did to Israel.

The regulations for wars other than those commanded in the Torah (190) are to be observed, and a priest must be (191) appointed for special duties in times of war. The military camp must be (192) kept in a sanitary condition. To this end, every soldier must be (193) equipped with the necessary implements.

Stolen property must be (194) restored to its owner. Give (195) charity to the poor. When a Hebrew slave goes free the owner must (196) give him gifts. Lend to (197) the poor without interest; to the foreigner you may (198) lend at interest. Restore (199) a pledge to its owner if he needs it. Pay the worker his wages (200) on time; (201) permit him to eat of the produce with which he is working. You must (202) help unload an animal when necessary, and also (203) help load human or beast [of burden]. Lost property (204) must be restored to its owner. You are required (205) to reprove the sinner, but you must (206) love your neighbor as yourself. You are instructed (207) to love the proselyte. Your weights and measures (208) must be accurate.

Respect the (209) wise; (210) honor and (211) revere your parents. You must (212) perpetuate the human species by marrying (213) according to the law. A bridegroom is to (214) rejoice with his bride for one year. Male children must (215) be circumcised. Should a man die childless, his brother must either (216) marry his widow or (217) release her (*chalitzah*). He who violates a virgin must (218) marry her and may never divorce her. If a man unjustly accuses his wife of premarital promiscuity (219), he shall be flogged, and may never divorce her. The seducer (220) must be punished according to the law. The female captive must be (221) treated in accordance with her special regulations. Divorce can be executed (222) only by means of a written document (*get*). A woman suspected of adultery (223) has to submit to the required test.

When required by the law, (224) you must administer the punishment of flogging and you must (225) exile the unwitting homicide. Capital punishment shall be by (226) the sword, (227) strangulation, (228) fire, or (229) stoning, as specified. In some cases the body of the executed (230) shall be hanged, but it (231) must be brought to burial the same day.

Hebrew slaves (232) must be treated according to the special laws for them. The master is to (233) marry his Hebrew maidservant or (234) redeem her. The alien slave (235) must be treated according to the regulations applying to him.

The applicable law must be administered in the case of injury caused by (236) a person, (237) an animal, or (238) a pit. Thieves (239) must be punished. You must render judgment in cases of (240) trespass by cattle, (241) arson, (242) embezzlement by an unpaid guardian, and in claims against (243) a paid guardian, a hirer, or (244) a borrower. Judgment must also be rendered in disputes arising out of (245) sales, (246) inheritance, and (247) other matters generally. You are required to (248) rescue the persecuted even if it means killing the oppressor.

Prohibitions

It is (1) forbidden to believe in the existence of any but the One God.

You may not make images (2) for yourself or (3) for others to worship or for (4) any other purpose.

You must not worship anything but God either in (5) the manner prescribed for Divine worship or (6) in its own manner of worship.

Do not (7) sacrifice children to Molech.

You may not (8) practice necromancy or (9) resort to familiar spirits; neither should you take idolatry or its mythology (10) seriously.

It is forbidden to construct a (11) pillar or (12) dais even for the worship of God or to (13) plant trees in the Temple.

You may not (14) swear by idols or instigate an idolater to do so, nor may you encourage or persuade any (15) non-Jew or (16) Jew to worship idols.

You must not (17) listen to or love anyone who disseminates idolatry, nor (18) should you withhold yourself from hating him [or her]. Do not (19) pity such a person. If somebody tries to convert you to idolatry (20), do not defend that person or (21) conceal the fact.

It is forbidden to (22) derive any benefit from the ornaments of idols. You may not (23) rebuild what has been destroyed as a punishment for idolatry, nor may you (24) gain any benefit from its wealth. Do not (25) use anything connected with idols or idolatry.

It is forbidden (26) to prophesy in the name of idols or to prophesy (27) falsely in the name of God. Do not (28) listen to the one who prophesies for idols, and do not (29) fear the false prophet or hinder his execution.

You must not (30) imitate the ways of idolaters or practice their customs; (31) divination, (32) soothsaying, (33) enchanting, (34) sorcery, (35) charming, (36) consulting ghosts or (37) familiar spirits, and (38) necromancy are forbidden. Women must not (39) wear male clothing nor men [clothing] (40) of women. Do not (41) tattoo yourself in the manner of the idolaters.

You may not wear (42) garments made of both wool and linen, nor may you shave [with a razor] the sides of (43) your head or (44) your beard. Do not (45) lacerate yourself over your dead.

It is forbidden to return to Egypt to (46) dwell there permanently or to (47) indulge in impure thoughts or sights. You may not (48) make a pact with the seven Canaanite nations or (49) save the life of any member of them. Do not (50) show mercy to idolaters, (51) permit them to dwell in the land of Israel, or (52) intermarry with them. A Jewish woman may not (53) marry an Ammonite or Moabite even if he converts to Judaism, and is to refuse [for reasons of genealogy alone] (54) a descendant of Esau or (55) an Egyptian who is a proselyte. It is prohibited to make (56) peace with the Ammonite or Moabite nation.

The (57) destruction of fruit trees even in times of war is forbidden, as is wanton waste at any time. Do not (58) fear the enemy and do not (59) forget the evil done by Amalek.

You must not (60) blaspheme the Holy Name, (61) break an oath made by it, (62) take it in vain, or (63) profane it. Do not (64) test Adonai, [who is] God.

You may not (65) erase God's name from the holy texts or destroy institutions devoted to Divine worship. Do not (66) allow the body of one hanged to remain so overnight.

Be not (67) lax in guarding the Temple.

The high priest must not enter the Temple (68) indiscriminately; a priest with a physical blemish may not (69) enter there at all or (70) serve in the sanctuary, and even if the blemish is of a temporary nature, he may not (71) participate in the service there until it has passed.

The Levites and the priests must not (72) interchange in their functions. Intoxicated persons may not (73) enter the sanctuary or teach the Torah. It is forbidden for (74) non-priests, (75) unclean priests, or (76) priests who have performed the necessary ablution but are still within the time limit of their uncleanness to serve in the Temple. No unclean person may enter (77) the Temple or (78) the Temple Mount.

The altar must not be made of (79) hewn stones, nor may the ascent to it be by (80) steps. The fire on it may not be (81) extinguished, nor may any other but the specified incense be (82) burned on the golden altar. You may not (83) manufacture oil with the same ingredients and in the same proportions as the anointing oil, which itself (84) may not be misused. Neither may you (85) compound incense with the same ingredients and in the same proportions as that burned on the altar. You must not (86) remove the staves from the Ark, (87) remove the breastplate from the ephod, or (88) make any incision in the upper garment of the high priest.

It is forbidden to (89) offer sacrifices or (90) slaughter consecrated animals outside the Temple. You may not (91) sanctify, (92) slaughter, (93) sprinkle the blood of, or (94) burn the inner parts of a blemished animal even if the blemish is (95) of a temporary nature and even if it is (96) offered by Gentiles. It is forbidden to (97) inflict a blemish on an animal consecrated for sacrifice.

Leaven or honey may not (98) be offered on the altar, neither may (99) anything unsalted. An animal received as the hire of a harlot or as the price of a dog (100) may not be offered.

Do not (101) kill an animal and its young on the same day.

It is forbidden to use (102) olive oil or (103) frankincense in the sin-offering or (104), (105) in the jealousy-offering (*sotah*). You may not (106) substitute sacrifices even (107) from one category to the other. You may not (108) redeem the firstborn of permitted animals. It is forbidden to (109) sell the tithe of the herd or (110) sell or (111) redeem a field consecrated by the *cherem* vow. When you slaughter a bird for a sin-offering you may not (112) split its head.

It is forbidden to (113) work with or (114) shear a consecrated animal. You must not slaughter the paschal lamb (115) while there is still leaven about; nor may you leave overnight (116) those parts that are to be offered up or (117) to be eaten.
You may not leave any part of the festive offering (118) until the third day or any part of (119) the second paschal lamb or (120) the thanksgiving-offering until the morning.

It is forbidden to break a bone of (121) the first or (122) second paschal lamb or (123) to carry their flesh out of the house where it is being eaten. You must not (124) allow the remains of the meal-offering to become leaven. It is also forbidden to eat the paschal lamb (125) raw or sodden or to allow (126) an alien resident, (127) an uncircumcised person, or an (128) apostate to eat of it.

A ritually unclean person (129) must not eat of holy

things, nor may (130) holy things which have become un-clean be eaten. Sacrificial meat (131) which is left after the time-limit or (132) which was slaughtered with wrong intentions must not be eaten. The heave-offering must not be eaten by (133) a non-priest, (134) a priest's sojourner or hired worker, (135) an uncircumcised person, or (136) an unclean priest. The daughter of a priest who is married to a non-priest may not (137) eat of holy things.

The meal-offering of the priest (138) must not be eaten, neither may (139) the flesh of the sin-offerings sacrificed within the sanctuary or (140) consecrated animals which have become blemished. You may not eat the second tithe of (141) corn, (142) wine, or (143) oil or (144) unblem-ished firstlings outside Jerusalem. The priests may not eat the (145) sin-offerings or the trespass-offerings outside the Temple courts or (146) the flesh of the burnt-offering at all. The lighter sacrifices (147) may not be eaten before the blood has been sprinkled. A non-priest may not (148) eat of the holiest sacrifices, and a priest (149) may not eat the first fruits outside the Temple courts.

One may not eat (150) the second tithe while in a state of impurity or (151) in mourning; its redemption money (152) may not be used for anything other than food and drink.

You must not (153) eat untithed produce or (154) change the order of separating the various tithes.

Do not (155) delay payment of offerings—either freewill or obligatory—and do not (156) come to the Temple on the pilgrim festivals without an offering.

Do not (157) break your word.

A priest may not marry (158) a harlot, (159) a woman who has been profaned from the priesthood, or (160) a divorcee; the high priests must not (161) marry a widow or (162) take one as a concubine. Priests may not enter the sanctuary with (163) overgrown hair of the head or (164) with torn clothing; they must not (165) leave the courtyard during the Temple service. An ordinary priest may not ren-der himself (166) ritually impure except for those relatives specified, and the high priest must not become impure (167) for anyone in (168) any way.

The tribe of Levi shall have no part in (169) the division of the land of Israel or (170) in the spoils of war.

It is forbidden (171) to make oneself bald as a sign of

mourning for one's dead.

A Jew may not eat (172) unclean cattle, (173) unclean fish, (174) unclean fowl, (175) creeping things that fly, (176) creatures that creep on the ground, (177) reptiles, (178) worms found in fruit or produce, or (179) any detestable creature.

An animal that dies naturally (180) is forbidden for consumption, as is (181) a torn or mauled animal. One must not eat (182) any limb taken from a living animal. Also prohibited is (183) the sinew of the thigh (*gid ha'nasheh*), as is (184) blood and (185) certain types of fat (*chelev*). It is forbidden (186) to cook meat together with milk or (187) to eat of such a mixture. It is also forbidden to eat (188) of an ox condemned to stoning (even should it have been properly slaughtered).

One may not eat (189) bread made of new corn or the new corn itself, either (190) roasted or (191) green, before the *omer* offering has been brought on the sixteenth of Nisan. You may not eat (192) *orlah* or (193) the growth of mixed planting in the vineyard. Any use of (194) wine libations to idols is prohibited, as is (195) gluttony and drunkenness. One may not eat anything on (196) the Day of Atonement. During Passover it is forbidden to eat (197) leaven (*chametz*) or (198) anything containing a mixture of such. This is also forbidden (199) after the middle of the fourteenth of Nisan [the day before Passover]. During Passover no leaven may be (200) seen or (201) found in your possession.

A Nazirite may not drink (202) wine or any beverage made from grapes; he may not eat (203) grapes, (204) dried grapes, (205) grape seeds, or (206) grape peel. He may not render himself (207) ritually impure for his dead, nor may he (208) enter a tent in which there is a corpse. He must not (209) shave his hair.

It is forbidden (210) to reap the whole of a field without leaving the corners for the poor; it is also forbidden to (211) gather up the ears of corn that fall during reaping or to harvest (212) the misformed clusters of grapes, or (213) the grapes that fall or to (214) return to take a forgotten sheaf.

You must not (215) sow different species of seed together or (216) corn in a vineyard; it is also forbidden to (217) crossbreed different species of animals or (218) work with two different species yoked together.

You must not (219) muzzle an animal working in a field to prevent it from eating.

It is forbidden to (220) till the earth, (221) to prune trees, (222) to reap [in the usual manner] produce or (223) fruit which has grown without cultivation in the seventh year (*shemittah*). One may also not (224) till the earth or prune trees in the Jubilee year, when it is also forbidden to harvest [in the usual manner] (225) produce or (226) fruit that has grown without cultivation.

One may not (227) sell one's landed inheritance in the land of Israel permanently or (228) change the lands of the Levites or (229) leave the Levites without support.

It is forbidden to (230) demand repayment of a loan after the seventh year; you may not, however, (231) refuse to lend to the poor because that year is approaching. Do not (232) deny charity to the poor or (233) send a Hebrew slave away empty-handed when he finishes his period of service. Do not (234) dun your debtor when you know that he [or she] cannot pay. It is forbidden to (235) lend to or (236) borrow from another Jew at interest or (237) to participate in an agreement involving interest either as a guarantor, witness, or writer of the contract.

Do not (238) delay in the payment of wages.

You may not (239) take a pledge from a debtor by violence, (240) keep a poor person's pledge when he [or she] needs it, (241) take any pledge from a widow or (242) from any debtor if he [or she] earns a living from it.

Kidnapping (243) a Jew is forbidden.

Do not (244) steal or (245) rob by violence. Do not (246) remove a land marker or (247) defraud.

It is forbidden (248) to deny receipt of a loan or a deposit or (249) to swear falsely regarding another person's property.

You must not (250) deceive anyone in business. You may not (251) mislead a person even (252) verbally or (253) do him [or her] injury in trade.

You may not (254) return or (255) otherwise take advantage of a slave who has fled to the land of Israel from his master, even if his master is a Jew.

Do not (256) afflict the widow or the orphan. You may not (257) misuse or (258) sell a Hebrew slave; do not (259) treat him cruelly or (260) allow a heathen to mistreat him. You must not (261) sell your Hebrew maidservant or, if you marry her, (262) withhold food, clothing, and conjugal rights from her. You must not (263) sell a female captive or (264) treat her as a slave.

Do not covet (265) another person's possessions even if you are willing to pay for them. Even (266) the desire alone is forbidden.

A worker must not (267) cut down standing corn during his [or her] work or (268) take more fruit than he [or she] can eat.

One must not (269) turn away from a lost article which is to be returned to its owner, nor may you (270) refuse to help a person on an animal which is collapsing under its burden.

It is forbidden to (271) defraud with weights and measures or even (272) to possess inaccurate weights.

A judge must not (273) perpetrate injustice, (274) accept bribes, or be (275) partial or (276) afraid. He [or she] may (277) not favor the poor or (278) discriminate against the wicked; he [or she] should not (279) pity the condemned or (280) pervert the judgment of strangers or orphans.

It is forbidden to (281) hear one litigant without the other being present. A capital case cannot be decided by (282) a majority of one.

A judge must not (283) accept a colleague's opinion unless he [or she] is convinced of its correctness; it is forbidden to (284) appoint as a judge someone who is ignorant of the law.

Do not (285) give false testimony or accept (286) testimony from a wicked person or from (287) relatives of a person involved in the case. It is forbidden to pronounce judgment (288) on the basis of the testimony of one witness.

Do not (289) murder.

You must not convict on (290) circumstantial evidence alone.

A witness (291) must not sit as a judge in capital cases. You must not (292) execute anyone without due proper trial and conviction.

Do not (293) pity or spare the pursuer.

Punishment is not to be inflicted for (294) an act committed under duress.

Do not accept ransom (295) for a murderer or (296) a manslayer.

Do not (297) hesitate to save another person from danger, and do not (298) leave a stumbling block in the way or (299) mislead another person by giving wrong advice.

It is forbidden (300) to administer more than the assigned number of lashes to the guilty.

Do not (301) tell tales or (302) bear hatred in your heart. It is forbidden to (303) shame a Jew, (304) to bear a grudge, or (305) to take revenge.

Do not (306) take the mother when you take the young birds.

It is forbidden to (307) shave a leprous scale or (308) remove other signs of that affliction. It is forbidden (309) to cultivate a valley in which a slain body was found and in which subsequently the ritual of breaking the heifer's neck (*egla arufah*) was performed.

Do not (310) suffer a witch to live.

Do not (311) force a bridegroom to perform military service during the first year of his marriage. It is forbidden to (312) rebel against the transmitters of the tradition or to (313) add or (314) detract from the precepts of the Torah.

Do not curse (315) a judge, (316) a ruler, or (317) any Jew. Do not (318) curse or (319) strike a parent.

It is forbidden to (320) work on the Sabbath or (321) to walk farther than the permitted limits (*eruv*). You may not (322) inflict punishment on the Sabbath.

It is forbidden to work on (323) the first or (324) the seventh day of Passover, on (325) Shavuot, on (326) Rosh Hashanah, on the (327) first and (328) eighth (*Shemini Atzeret*) days of Sukkot, and (329) on the Day of Atonement.

It is forbidden to enter into an incestuous relationship with one's (330) mother, (331) stepmother, (332) sister, (333) half-sister, (334) son's daughter, (335) daughter's daughter, (336) daughter, (337) any woman and her daughter, (338) any woman and her son's daughter, (339) any woman and her daughter's daughter, (340) father's sister, (341) mother's sister, (342) paternal uncle's wife, (343) daughter-in-law, (344) brother's wife, or (345) wife's sister.

It is also forbidden to (346) have sexual relations with a menstruous woman.

Do not (347) commit adultery.

It is forbidden for (348) a man or (349) a woman to have sexual intercourse with an animal.

Homosexuality (350) is forbidden, particularly with (351) one's father or (352) uncle.

It is forbidden to have (353) intimate physical contact (even without actual intercourse) with any of the women with whom intercourse is forbidden.

A *mamzer* (illegitimate child) may not marry (354) a Jewish woman.

Prostitution (355) is forbidden.

A divorcee may not be (356) remarried to her first husband if, in the meanwhile, she had married another.

A childless widow may not (357) marry anyone other than her late husband's brother.

A man may not (358) divorce a wife whom he married after having raped her or (359) after having slandered her.

A eunuch may not (360) marry a Jewish woman.

Castration (361) is forbidden.

You may not (362) elect as king anyone who is not of the seed of Israel.

The king may not accumulate an excessive number of (363) horses, (364) wives, or (365) wealth.

Things to remember:

1. There are 248 positive instructions (in other words, things that we are supposed to do) and 365 negative instructions (or things we are prohibited from doing).

2. According to traditional Jewish law, women were exempt from performing any *mitzvah* that had to be done at a specific time (with exceptions, including the lighting of Sabbath candles).

3. The first attempt at classifying all of the commandments was made in the *Halachot Gedolot* by Rabbi Simeon Kahira (8th cent. C.E.). His example was followed by many others, including Rabbi Saadia Gaon and Maimonides.

4. In Jewish law, boys at thirteen and girls at twelve become subject to the performance of the commandments.

5. There is a tradition that 611 of the 613 commandments were given through Moses (and the other two, the first and second of the Ten Commandments, directly by God

at Mount Sinai). The basis for this tradition is the fact that the numerical value of the word *torah* (תּוֹרָה) is 611. For further discussion of this method of interpretation, see the discussion of gematria on p. 32.

Biblical Sources:

Textual Sources for Positive Commandments

1. Exodus 20:2   2. Deuteronomy 6:4   3. Deuteronomy 6:13   4. Deuteronomy 6:13   5. Exodus 23:25; Deuteronomy 11:13; (Deuteronomy 6:13 and 13:5)   6. Deuteronomy 10:20   7. Deuteronomy 19:20   8. Deuteronomy 28:9   9. Leviticus 22:32   10. Deuteronomy 6:7   11. Deuteronomy 6:7   12. Deuteronomy 6:8   13. Deuteronomy 6:8   14. Numbers 15:38   15. Deuteronomy 6:9   16. Deuteronomy 31:12   17. Deuteronomy 17:18   18. Deuteronomy 31:19   19. Deuteronomy 8:10   20. Exodus 25:8   21. Leviticus 19:30   22. Numbers 18:4   23. Numbers 18:23   24. Exodus 30:19   25. Exodus 27:21   26. Numbers 6:23   27. Exodus 25:30   28. Exodus 30:7   29. Leviticus 6:6   30. Leviticus 6:3   31. Numbers 5:4   32. Leviticus 21:8   33. Exodus 28:2   34. Numbers 7:9   35. Exodus 30:31   36. Deuteronomy 18:6-8   37. Leviticus 21:2-3   38. Leviticus 21:13   39. Numbers 28:3   40. Leviticus 6:13   41. Numbers 28:9   42. Numbers 28:11   43. Leviticus 23:26   44. Leviticus 23:10   45. Numbers 28:26-27   46. Leviticus 23:17   47. Numbers 29:1-2   48. Numbers 28:26-27   49. Leviticus 16   50. Numbers 29:13   51. Numbers 29:36   52. Exodus 23:14   53. Exodus 34:23; Deuteronomy 16:16   54. Deuteronomy 16:14   55. Exodus 12:6   56. Exodus 12:8   57. Numbers 9:11   58. Numbers 9:11; Exodus 12:8   59. Numbers 10:10; 10:9   60. Leviticus 22:27   61. Leviticus 22:21   62. Leviticus 2:13   63. Leviticus 1:2   64. Leviticus 6:18   65. Leviticus 7:1   66. Leviticus 3:1   67. Leviticus 2:1; 6:7   68. Leviticus 4:13   69. Leviticus 4:27   70. Leviticus 5:17-18   71. Leviticus 5:15, 21-25; 19:20-21   72. Leviticus 5:1-11   73. Numbers 5:6-7   74. Leviticus 15:13-15   75. Leviticus 15:28-29   76. Leviticus 12:6   77. Leviticus 14:10   78. Leviticus 27:32   79. Exodus 13:2   80. Exodus 22:28; Numbers 18:15   81. Exodus 34:20   82. Exodus 13:13   83. Deuteronomy 12:5   84. Deuteronomy 12:14   85. Deuteronomy 12:26   86. Deuteronomy 12:15   87. Leviticus 27:33   88. Leviticus 8:9   89. Exodus 29:33   90. Leviticus 7:19   91. Leviticus 7:17   92. Numbers 6:5   93. Numbers 6:18   94. Deuteronomy 23:24   95. Numbers 30:3   96. Leviticus 11:8, 24   97. Leviticus 11:29-31   98. Leviticus 11:34   99. Leviticus 15:19   100. Leviticus 12:2   101. Leviticus 13:3   102. Leviticus 13:51   103. Leviticus 14:44   104. Leviticus 15:2   105. Leviticus 15:16   106. Leviticus 15:19   107. Numbers 19:14   108. Numbers 19:13, 21   109. Leviticus 15:16   110. Leviticus 14:2   111. Leviticus 14:9   112. Leviticus 13:45   113. Numbers 19:2-9   114. Leviticus 27:2-8   115. Leviticus 27:11-12

116. Leviticus 27:14   117. Leviticus 27:16, 22-23   118. Leviticus 5:16   119. Leviticus 19:24   120. Leviticus 19:9   121. Leviticus 19:9   122. Deuteronomy 24:19   123. Leviticus 19:10   124. Leviticus 19:10   125. Exodus 23:19   126. Deuteronomy 18:4   127. Leviticus 27:30; Numbers 18:24   128. Deuteronomy 14:22   129. Numbers 18:26   130. Deuteronomy 14:28   131. Deuteronomy 26:13   132. Deuteronomy 26:5   133. Numbers 15:20   134. Exodus 23:11   135. Exodus 34:21   136. Leviticus 25:10   137. Leviticus 25:9   138. Leviticus 25:24   139. Leviticus 25:29-30   140. Leviticus 25:8   141. Deuteronomy 15:3   142. Deuteronomy 15:3   143. Deuteronomy 18:3   144. Deuteronomy 18:4   145. Leviticus 27:21, 28   146. Deuteronomy 12:21   147. Leviticus 17:13   148. Deuteronomy 22:7   149. Leviticus 11:2   150. Deuteronomy 14:11   151. Leviticus 11:21   152. Leviticus 11:9   153. Exodus 12:2; Deuteronomy 16:1   154. Exodus 23:12   155. Exodus 20:8   156. Exodus 12:15   157. Exodus 13:8   158. Exodus 12:8   159. Exodus 12:16   160. Exodus 12:16   161. Leviticus 23:35   162. Leviticus 23   163. Leviticus 23:24   164. Leviticus 16:29   165. Leviticus 16:29,31   166. Leviticus 23:35   167. Leviticus 23:42   168. Leviticus 23:42   169. Leviticus 23:40   170. Numbers 29:1   171. Exodus 30:12-13   172. Deuteronomy 18:15   173. Deuteronomy 17:15   174. Deuteronomy 17:11   175. Exodus 23:2   176. Deuteronomy 16:18   177. Leviticus 19:15   178. Leviticus 5:1   179. Deuteronomy 13:15   180. Deuteronomy 19:19   181. Deuteronomy 21:4   182. Deuteronomy 19:3   183. Numbers 35:2   184. Deuteronomy 22:8   185. Deuteronomy 12:2; 7:5   186. Deuteronomy 13:17   187. Deuteronomy 20:17   188. Deuteronomy 25:19   189. Deuteronomy 25:17   190. Deuteronomy 20:11-12   191. Deuteronomy 20:2   192. Deuteronomy 23:14-15   193. Deuteronomy 23:14   194. Leviticus 5:23   195. Deuteronomy 15:8; Leviticus 25:35-36   196. Deuteronomy 15:14   197. Exodus 22:24   198. Deuteronomy 23:21   199. Deuteronomy 24:13; Exodus 22:25   200. Deuteronomy 24:15   201. Deuteronomy 23:25-26   202. Exodus 23:5   203. Deuteronomy 22:4   204. Deuteronomy 22:1; Exodus 23:4   205. Leviticus 19:17   206. Leviticus 19:18   207. Deuteronomy 10:19   208. Leviticus 19:36   209. Leviticus 19:32   210. Exodus 20:12   211. Leviticus 19:3   212. Genesis 1:28   213. Deuteronomy 24:1   214. Deuteronomy 24:5   215. Genesis 17:10; Leviticus 12:3   216. Deuteronomy 25:5   217. Deuteronomy 25:9   218. Deuteronomy 22:29   219. Deuteronomy 22:18-19   220. Exodus 22:15-23   221. Deuteronomy 21:11   222. Deuteronomy 24:1   223. Numbers 5:15-27   224. Deuteronomy 25:2   225. Numbers 35:25   226. Exodus 21:20   227. Exodus 21:16   228. Leviticus 20:14   229. Deuteronomy 22:24   230. Deuteronomy 21:22   231. Deuteronomy 21:23   232. Exodus 21:2   233. Exodus 21:8   234. Exodus 21:8   235. Leviticus 25:46   236. Exodus 21:18   237. Exodus 21:28   238. Exodus 21:33–34   239. Exodus 21:37,

22:3   240. Exodus 22:4   241. Exodus 22:5   242. Exodus 22:6-8   243. Exodus 22:9-12   244. Exodus 22:13   245. Leviticus 25:14   246. Exodus 22:8   247. Deuteronomy 25:12   248. Numbers 27:8

Textual Sources for Prohibitions

1. Exodus 20:3   2. Exodus 20:4   3. Leviticus 19:4   4. Exodus 20:20   5. Exodus 20:5   6. Exodus 20:5   7. Leviticus 18:21   8. Leviticus 19:31   9. Leviticus 19:31   10. Leviticus 19:4   11. Deuteronomy 16:21   12. Leviticus 20:1   13. Deuteronomy 16:21   14. Exodus 23:13   15. Exodus 23:13   16. Deuteronomy 13:12   17. Deuteronomy 13:9   18. Deuteronomy 13:9   19. Deuteronomy 13:9   20. Deuteronomy 13:9   21. Deuteronomy 13:9   22. Deuteronomy 7:25   23. Deuteronomy 13:17   24. Deuteronomy 13:18   25. Deuteronomy 7:26   26. Deuteronomy 18:20   27. Deuteronomy 18:20   28. Deuteronomy 13:3–4   29. Deuteronomy 18:22   30. Leviticus 20:23   31. Leviticus 19:26; Deuteronomy 18:10   32. Deuteronomy 18:10   33. Deuteronomy 18:10-26   34. Deuteronomy 18:10-11   35. Deuteronomy 18:10-11   36. Deuteronomy 18:10-11   37. Deuteronomy 18:10-11   38. Deuteronomy 18:10-11   39. Deuteronomy 22:5   40. Deuteronomy 22:5   41. Leviticus 19:28   42. Deuteronomy 22:11   43. Leviticus 19:27   44. Leviticus 19:27   45. Deuteronomy 16:1; 14:1; Leviticus 19:28   46. Deuteronomy 17:16   47. Numbers 15:39   48. Exodus 23:32; Deuteronomy 7:2   49. Deuteronomy 20:16   50. Deuteronomy 7:2   51. Exodus 23:33   52. Deuteronomy 7:3   53. Deuteronomy 23:4   54. Deuteronomy 23:8   55. Deuteronomy 23:8   56. Deuteronomy 23:7   57. Deuteronomy 20:19   58. Deuteronomy 7:21   59. Deuteronomy 25:19   60. Leviticus 24:16; Exodus 22:27   61. Leviticus 19:12   62. Exodus 20:7   63. Leviticus 22:32   64. Deuteronomy 6:16   65. Deuteronomy 12:4   66. Deuteronomy 21:23   67. Numbers 18:5   68. Leviticus 16:2   69. Leviticus 21:23   70. Leviticus 21:17   71. Leviticus 21:18   72. Numbers 18:3   73. Leviticus 10:9-11   74. Numbers 18:4   75. Leviticus 22:2   76. Leviticus 21:6   77. Numbers 5:3   78. Deuteronomy 23:11   79. Exodus 20:25   80. Exodus 20:26   81. Leviticus 6:6   82. Exodus 30:9   83. Exodus 30:32   84. Exodus 30:32   85. Exodus 30:37   86. Exodus 25:15   87. Exodus 28:28   88. Exodus 28:32   89. Deuteronomy 12:13   90. Leviticus 17:3-4   91. Leviticus 22:20   92. Leviticus 22:22   93. Leviticus 22:24   94. Leviticus 22:22   95. Deuteronomy 17:1   96. Leviticus 22:25   97. Leviticus 22:21   98. Leviticus 2:11   99. Leviticus 2:13   100. Deuteronomy 23:19   101. Leviticus 22:28   102. Leviticus 5:11   103. Leviticus 5:11   104. Numbers 5:15   105. Numbers 5:15   106. Leviticus 27:10   107. Leviticus 27:26   108. Numbers 18:17   109. Leviticus 27:33   110. Leviticus 27:28   111. Leviticus 27:28   112. Leviticus 5:8   113. Deuteronomy 15:19   114. Deuteronomy 15:19   115. Exodus 34:25   116. Exodus 23:10   117. Exodus 12:10

118. Deuteronomy 16:4   119. Numbers 9:13   120. Leviticus 22:30   121. Exodus 12:46   122. Numbers 9:12   123. Exodus 12:46   124. Leviticus 6:10   125. Exodus 12:9   126. Exodus 12:45   127. Exodus 12:48   128. Exodus 12:43   129. Leviticus 12:4   130. Leviticus 7:19   131. Leviticus 19:6-8   132. Leviticus 7:18   133. Leviticus 22:10   134. Leviticus 22:10   135. Leviticus 22:10   136. Leviticus 22:4   137. Leviticus 22:12   138. Leviticus 6:16   139. Leviticus 6:23   140. Deuteronomy 14:3   141. Deuteronomy 12:17   142. Deuteronomy 12:17   143. Deuteronomy 12:17   144. Deuteronomy 12:17   145. Deuteronomy 12:17   146. Deuteronomy 12:17   147. Deuteronomy 12:17   148. Deuteronomy 12:17   149. Exodus 29:33   150. Deuteronomy 26:14   151. Deuteronomy 26:14   152. Deuteronomy 26:14   153. Leviticus 22:15   154. Exodus 22:28   155. Deuteronomy 23:22   156. Exodus 23:15   157. Numbers 30:3   158. Leviticus 21:7   159. Leviticus 21:7   160. Leviticus 21:7   161. Leviticus 21:14   162. Leviticus 21:15   163. Leviticus 10:6   164. Leviticus 10:6   165. Leviticus 10:7   166. Leviticus 21:1   167. Leviticus 21:11   168. Leviticus 21:11   169. Deuteronomy 18:1   170. Deuteronomy 18:1   171. Deuteronomy 14:1   172. Deuteronomy 14:7   173. Leviticus 11:11   174. Leviticus 11:13   175. Deuteronomy 14:19   176. Leviticus 11:41   177. Leviticus 11:44   178. Leviticus 11:42   179. Leviticus 11:43   180. Deuteronomy 14:21   181. Exodus 22:30   182. Deuteronomy 12:23   183. Genesis 32:33   184. Leviticus 7:26   185. Leviticus 7:23   186. Exodus 23:19   187. Exodus 34:26   188. Exodus 21:28   189. Leviticus 23:14   190. Leviticus 23:14   191. Leviticus 23:14   192. Leviticus 19:23   193. Deuteronomy 22:9   194. Deuteronomy 32:38   195. Leviticus 19:26; Deuteronomy 21:20   196. Leviticus 23: 29   197. Exodus 13:3   198. Exodus 13:20   199. Deuteronomy 16:3   200. Exodus 13:7   201. Exodus 12:19   202. Numbers 6:3   203. Numbers 6:3   204. Numbers 6:3   205. Numbers 6:4   206. Numbers 6:4   207. Numbers 6:7   208. Leviticus 21:11   209. Numbers 6:5   210. Leviticus 23:22   211. Leviticus 19:9   212. Leviticus 19:10   213. Leviticus 19:10   214. Deuteronomy 24:19   215. Leviticus 19:19   216. Deuteronomy 22:9   217. Leviticus 19:19   218. Deuteronomy 22:10   219. Deuteronomy 25:4   220. Leviticus 25:4   221. Leviticus 25:4   222. Leviticus 25:5   223. Leviticus 25:5   224. Leviticus 25:11   225. Leviticus 25:11   226. Leviticus 25:11   227. Leviticus 25:23   228. Leviticus 25:33   229. Deuteronomy 12:19   230. Deuteronomy 15:2   231. Deuteronomy 15:9   232. Deuteronomy 15:7   233. Deuteronomy 15:13   234. Exodus 22:24   235. Leviticus 25:37   236. Deuteronomy 23:20   237. Exodus 22:24   238. Leviticus 19:13   239. Deuteronomy 24:10   240. Deuteronomy 24:12   241. Deuteronomy 24:17   242. Deuteronomy 24:10   243. Exodus 20:13   244. Leviticus 19:11   245. Leviticus 19:13   246. Deuteronomy 19:14   247. Leviticus 19:13   248. Leviticus 19:11   249. Leviticus 19:11   250. Leviticus

25:14　251. Leviticus 25:17　252. Exodus 22:20　253. Exodus 22:20　254. Deuteronomy 23:16　255. Deuteronomy 23:17 256. Exodus 22:21　257. Leviticus 25:39　258. Leviticus 25:42 259. Leviticus 25:43　260. Leviticus 25:53　261. Exodus 21:8　262. Exodus 21:10　263. Deuteronomy 21:14 264. Deuteronomy 21:14　265. Exodus 20:17　266. Deuteronomy 5:18　267. Deuteronomy 23:26　268. Deuteronomy 23:25 269. Deuteronomy 22:　270. Exodus 23:5　271. Leviticus 19:35 272. Deuteronomy 25:13　273. Leviticus 19:15　274. Exodus 23:8 275. Leviticus 19:15　276. Deuteronomy 1:17　277. Leviticus 19:15: Exodus 23:3　278. Exodus 23:6　279. Deuteronomy 19:13 280. Deuteronomy 24:17　281. Exodus 23:1　282. Exodus 23:2 283. Exodus 23:2　284. Deuteronomy 1:17　285. Exodus 20:16　286. Exodus 23:1　287. Deuteronomy 24:16　288. Deuteronomy 19:15　289. Exodus 20:13　290. Exodus 23:7　291. Numbers 35:30　292. Numbers 35:12　293. Deuteronomy 25:12 294. Deuteronomy 22:26　295. Numbers 35:31　296. Numbers 35:32　297. Leviticus 19:16　298. Deuteronomy 22:8　299. Leviticus 19:14　300. Deuteronomy 25:2-3　301. Leviticus 19:16 302. Leviticus 19:17　303. Leviticus 19:17　304. Leviticus 19:18 305. Leviticus 19:18　306. Deuteronomy 22:6　307. Leviticus 13:33　308. Deuteronomy 24:8　309. Deuteronomy 21:4　310. Exodus 22:17　311. Deuteronomy 24:5　312. Deuteronomy 17:11 313. Deuteronomy 13:1　314. Deuteronomy 13:1　315. Exodus 22:27　316. Exodus 22:27　317. Leviticus 19:14　318. Exodus 21:17　319. Exodus 21:15　320. Exodus 20:10　321. Exodus 16:29　322. Exodus 35:3　323. Exodus 12:16　324. Exodus 12:16 325. Leviticus 23:21　326. Leviticus 23:25　327. Leviticus 23:35 328. Leviticus 23:36　329. Leviticus 23:28　330. Leviticus 18:7 331. Leviticus 18:8　332. Leviticus 18:9　333. Leviticus 18:11 334. Leviticus 18:10　335. Leviticus 18:10　336. Leviticus 18: 10 337. Leviticus 18:17　338. Leviticus 18:17　339. Leviticus 18:17 340. Leviticus 18:12　341. Leviticus 18:13　342. Leviticus 18:14 343. Leviticus 18:15　344. Leviticus 18:16　345. Leviticus 18:18 346. Leviticus 18:19　347. Leviticus 18:20　348. Leviticus 18:23 349. Leviticus 18:23　350. Leviticus 18:22　351. Leviticus 18:7 352. Leviticus 18:14　353. Leviticus 18:6　354. Deuteronomy 23:3 355. Deuteronomy 23:18　356. Deuteronomy 24:4　357. Deuteronomy 25:5　358. Deuteronomy 22:29　359. Deuteronomy 22:19 360. Deuteronomy 23:2　361. Leviticus 22:24　362. Deuteronomy 17:15　363. Deuteronomy 17:16　364. Deuteronomy 17:17 365. Deuteronomy 17:17

Key words and phrases:

Mitzvah מִצְוָה. (plural, *mitzvot* מִצְווֹת). Commandment (or instruction).

Mitzvat aseh מִצְוַת עֲשֵׂה. Positive commandment.

Mitzvat lo ta'aseh מִצְוַת לֹא תַעֲשֶׂה. Negative commandment.

Taryag mitzvot תַּרְיַ"ג מִצְוֹת. The 613 commandments; the word *taryag* is a mnemonic for remembering the number.

If you want to know more:

Gersion Appel, *A Philosophy of Mizvot* (Hoboken, NJ, 1975).

Philip Birnbaum, *A Book of Jewish Concepts* (New York, 1964).

Abraham Chill, *The Mitzvot* (New York, 1974).

Encyclopaedia Judaica (Jerusalem, 1975), 5:760 ff.

Aaron HaLevi, *The Book of Mitzvah Education*, 5 vols. (Jerusalem, 1978).

Ron Isaacs *The Book of Commandments: A Source Book* (Northvale, NJ, forthcoming).

Instant Information
Magazines, Newspapers and Journals

What you need to know:

Many of these periodicals are sponsored by religious or ideologically-based organizations. Thus, some of them express viewpoints different from those expressed by others on the same list. Taken together, however, these journals, magazines, and newspapers present a cross-section of the attitudes and opinions of Jews around the world. Thus, they are important for the modern Jew who wishes to function in the contemporary Jewish world.

Periodicals

AJS Review

Academic journal for members of the Association of Jewish Studies.

Brandeis University
Waltham, MA 02254

American Jewish Archives

Academic journal published by the institution of the same name, primarily devoted to the preservation and study of the American Jewish experience.

American Jewish Archives
3101 Clifton Avenue
Cincinnati, OH 45220

American Jewish History

Academic journal primarily devoted to the study of the American Jewish experience and sponsored by the American Jewish Historical Society.

American Jewish Historical Society
2 Thornton Road
Waltham, MA 02154

Biblical Archaeology Review

Independent and sometimes controversial magazine aimed at both general readers and those well-versed in archaeology.

Biblical Archaeology Society
4710 41st Street NW
Washington, DC 20016

CCAR Journal

Professional journal of the Central Conference of American Rabbis, the international organization of Reform rabbis.

Central Conference of American Rabbis
192 Lexington Avenue
New York, NY 10016

Commentary

Generally representing a politically conservative point of view; sponsored by the American Jewish Committee.

American Jewish Committee
165 East 65th Street
New York, NY 10022

Congress Monthly

Sponsored by the American Jewish Congress, historically a liberal organization.

American Jewish Congress
15 East 84th Street
New York, NY 10028

Conservative Judaism

Professional journal of Rabbinical Assembly of America, the international organization of Conservative rabbis.

Rabbinical Assembly of America
3080 Broadway
New York, NY 10027

Cross-Currents

Interfaith publication sponsored by Association for Religion and Intellectual Life.

Association for Religion and Intellectual Life
College of New Rochelle
New Rochelle, NY 10805

Dimensions

Holocaust education publication of Anti-Defamation League of B'nai B'rith and its Braun Center for Holocaust Studies.

Anti-Defamation League
823 United Nations Plaza
New York, NY 10017

European Judaism

Published in association with Leo Baeck College, the liberal rabbinical training institution in London, and the Michael Goulston Education Foundation.

The Manor House
80 East End Road
London N32SY
United Kingdom

Hadassah

House organ of the women's Zionist organization, includes excellent articles on education and parenting.

Hadassah
50 West 58th Street
New York, NY 10019

Humanistic Judaism

House organ of Society for Humanistic Judaism.

Society for Humanistic Judaism
28611 West Twelve Mile Road
Farmington Hills, MI 48334

Jerusalem Report

Leading popular Jewish periodical today, covering Israel and the Middle East.

Jerusalem Report
1212 Avenue of the Americas
New York, NY 10036
or 22 Rehov Yosef Rivlin
Jerusalem 91017 Israel

National Jewish Monthly

Sponsored by B'nai B'rith International; easy-to-read magazine with information about popular Jewish culture.

B'nai B'rith International
1640 Rhode Island Avenue
Washington, DC 20036

Jewish Quarterly

Arts and literature journal.

Jewish Quarterly
P.O. Box 1148
London NW5 ZAZ
United Kingdom

Jewish Spectator

Excellent thinker's magazine with a long track record, founded by Trude Weiss-Rosmarin.

American Friends of the Center
for Jewish Living and Values
4391 Park Milana
Calabasas, CA 91302

Journal of Psychology and Judaism

Independent journal edited by a rabbi, with an excellent annual issue on aging.

Human Sciences Press
233 Spring Street
New York, NY 10013

Judaism

Sponsored by American Jewish Congress and representing a wide perspective of opinions.

American Jewish Congress
15 East 84th Street
New York, NY 10028

Lilith

Leading Jewish feminist magazine.

Lilith
250 West 57th Street
New York, NY 10107

Midstream

General journal on Zionism.

Theodor Herzl Foundation
110 East 57th Street
New York, NY 10022

Moment

Independent magazine, founded by Leonard Fein, features popular articles about contemporary Jewish culture.

Jewish Educational Ventures
4710 41st Street NW
Washington, DC 20016

Near-East Report

Weekly report out of Washington on American Middle Eastern policy.

Near East Research
440 First Street NW, Suite 607
Washington, DC 20001

Reconstructionist

House organ of Reconstructionist movement, published by its rabbinical college.

Reconstructionist Rabbinical College
Church Road and Greenwood Avenue
Wyncote, PA 19095

Reform Judaism

House organ of Union of American Hebrew Congregations, national organization of Reform synagogues.

Union of American Hebrew Congregations
838 Fifth Avenue
New York, NY 10021

Sh'ma: A Journal of Jewish Responsibility

Started by philosopher/theologian Eugene B. Borowitz, now published by CLAL (Center for Jewish Learning and Leadership).

CLAL
99 Park Avenue South, Suite 300
New York, NY

Tikkun

Relatively young publication, edited by Michael Lerner, representing a liberal political perspective.

Tikkun
P.O. Box 1758 Cathedral Station
New York, NY 10025

Torah Umada'a Journal

Orthodox journal about Jewish law, sponsored by the rabbinical seminary at Yeshiva University.

Rabbi Isaac Elchanan Theological Seminary
500 West 185th Street
New York, NY 10033

Tradition

Orthodox journal of thought sponsored by the Rabbinical Council of America, a centrist Orthodox rabbinical organization.

Rabbinical Council of America
275 Seventh Avenue
New York, NY 10011

United Synagogue Review

House organ of United Synagogue for Conservative Judaism, the national organization of Conservative synagogues.

United Synagogue for Conservative Judaism
155 Fifth Avenue
New York, NY 10010

Newspapers

Forward

The newspaper that Americanized your grandparents and great-grandparents, while teaching them English at the same time. In its current form, it is geared to young intellectuals.

44 East 33rd Street
New York, NY 10016

Jerusalem Post

The only English-language daily in Israel, also available in a weekend overseas edition, this newspaper has become very right wing since it changed ownership several years ago.

6 Oholiav Street
Jerusalem 91000
211 East 43rd Street, Suite 601
New York, NY 10017

(Philadelphia) Jewish Exponent

Excellent community newspaper.

226 South 16th Street
Philadelphia, PA 19102

(National) Jewish Post and Opinion

National newspaper with regional editions, of limited journalistic quality.

611 North Park Avenue
Indianapolis, IN 46204

(Baltimore) Jewish Times

Excellent local newspaper.

2104 North Charles Street
Baltimore, MD 21218

(New York) Jewish Week

Keeps you informed about the largest Jewish community in North America.

3 East 40th Street
New York, NY 10016

If you want to know more:

The Jewish Telegraphic Agency (JTA) keeps you informed about things taking place in the Jewish world. While many local Jewish papers carry material from JTA, you can subscribe directly.

Jewish Telegraphic Agency
165 West 46th Street, Room 511
New York, NY 10036

Instant Information
Videos and Video Distributors

What you need to know:

There are literally hundreds of videos of Jewish interest available at your local video store; there are also distributors which specialize in Jewish content and interest. We are including some of these distributors below. Try your local Bureau of Jewish Education or local Jewish book store, especially if you live in a large metropolitan area. But don't forget, everyone has a telephone!

If you want to know more:

1. For fun, why not try studying the Bible by watching a good video? Here are some titles to look for:

> *Queen Esther,* starring Victoria Principal
> *Samson and Delilah,* starring Joan Collins
> *Samson and Delilah* with Victor Mature and Hedy Lamar
> *Solomon and Sheba* with Yul Brynner
> *David and Bathsheba* with Gregory Peck
> *King David,* starring Richard Gere
> *The Ten Commandments,* directed by Cecil B. De Mille

2. You'll also want to look for classics like *Cast a Giant Shadow,* starring Kirk Douglas; *Exodus,* starring Paul Newman; and *Marjorie Morningstar,* with Natalie Wood and Gene Kelly.

3. Hanna Barbera has a modest series of children's Bible cartoons, called *The Greatest Adventure,* available through:
UAHC Television and Film Institute
838 Fifth Avenue
New York, NY 10021
or
Hanna-Barbera
3900 Cahuenga Boulevard
Hollywood, CA 90068

Rabbit Ears Productions (of Rowayton, CT) also has an excellent Bible story series (called *The Greatest Stories Ever Told*), read by actors and actresses, like *Noah and the Ark* read by Kelly McGillis.

4. Don't forget the Israeli *Sesame Street* program, which has been adapted for American distribution under the *Shalom Sesame* label. Two volumes (on holidays and places of interest in Israel) are available.

5. Companies well known for their ability to put award-winning children's books on films have many tapes of Jewish interest, like Barbara Cohen's *Molly's Pilgrim* and Isaac Bashevis Singer's *Zlateh the Goat*. Many are available from:
Weston Woods
Weston, CT 06883

6. Here are some films that made it to the big screen and are now available in video. When you are looking for a film for a Saturday night at home, why not rent one of the following:

> *Au Revoir les Enfants*
> *The Boat Is Full*
> *The Boys from Brazil*
> *The Chosen*
> *Crossing Delancey*
> *The Delta Force*
> *Hanna's War*
> *Hester Street*
> *Judgment at Nuremberg*
> *Music Box*
> *Oh God (I and II)*
> *Raid on Entebbe*

7. Here are some children's films to look for that may have been broadcast over your local PBS or Disney station:

> *An American Tale*
> *The Animated Haggadah*
> *Lights*

8. These were made for TV:

> *Holocaust*

The House on Garibaldi Street
The Impossible Spy
Operation Thunderbolt

10. There are some which only made it to the arts cinemas, like *Wedding in Galilee*.

More particulars:

For more specific information, contact:

Columbia House Video Library
(including *Masters of the Bible* series)
1-800-638-2922

Ergo Media
668 Front Street
P.O. Box 2037
Teaneck, NJ 07666

Jewish Educational Video
713 Crown Street
Brooklyn, NY 10010

Jewish Video Library
300 Raritan Avenue
Highland Park, NJ 08904

National Center for Jewish Film
Lown Building 102
Brandeis University
Waltham, MA 02254

Sisu Home Entertainment
475 Fifth Avenue, 23rd Floor
New York, NY 10017

Instant Information
The Electronic Arts

What you need to know:

Please note: Much of this material is for the serious student and often quite expensive. Some of the material requires Hebrew language skills. [The material in this chapter was prepared with the assistance of Professor Marc Bregman, Hebrew Union College–Jewish Institute of Religion, Jerusalem.]

CD-ROM and Hard Disk

CD-ROM Judaic Classics Library, *Babylonian Talmud*, Soncino Edition (Hebrew and English)
for MAC or PC with windows, Davka Corporation

Midrash Rabbah, Soncino Edition (Hebrew and English) on CD-ROM, Davka Corporation

ServiceMaker—program for creating liturgies
designed and distributed by Joel M. Hoffman (joel@wam.umd.edu)

Talmud Text Data Bank (Hebrew)
Index of references dealing with talmudic literature
Line Collation Software,
Saul Lieberman Institute of Talmudic Research, Jewish Theological Seminary of America

Bar-Ilan University Responsa Project (Hebrew)
Includes Bible, Commentaries, Talmuds, Midrash, Poskim, and Responsa
distributed in the United States by Torah Educational Software

If you want to know more:

Internet

Libraries (on-line catalogs and data bases):

Harvard University
telnet hollis.harvard.educ or telnet 128.103.60.31

University of California
telnet melvyl.ucop.edc or telnet 192.35.222.222

ALEPH (Israel University Libraries)
telnet aleph.huji.ac.il or telnet 128.139.4.15
telnet ram2.huji.ac.il or telnet 128.139.4.3
Data bases:
RAMBI (Index to Articles in Jewish Studies) [LB/JNL.RBI]
IHP (Index to Hebrew Periodicals) [LB/IHP]—includes all Israeli newspapers

Uncover (article access and delivery by fax)/fee for service
E-mail: database@carl.org, tel. 303/758-3030

Jewish Networks

SHAMASH: Jewish Networking Project
(gopher israel.nysernet.org)

Jerusalem One: Global Jewish Networking
(gopher jerusalem1.datasrv.co.il)

Discussion Groups, Forums, Lists

Clari.News.Jews: ClariNet wire service articles about Jewish matters/ fee for service
    (info@clarinet.com)
Ioudaios: Judaism in the Greco-Roman world
    (ioudaios-l@lehigh.edu)
Israeline: Israel press clippings via the Israeli Consulate in New York
    (nycon@israel-info.gov.il)
Israel-Mideast: information and editorials from the Israeli press via Foreign Ministry
    (analysis%israel-infor.gov.il@vm.tau.ac.il)
Jewish-psy: Judaism and mental health
    (Jewish-psy@jerusalem1.datasrv.co.il)
PJAL: Discussion forum for progressive Jews
    (pjal@israel.nysernet.ORG)
PJML: Discussion forum for progressive Jews
    (pjml@israel.nysernet.ORG)
Postmodern Jewish Philosophy Network
    (Journal: pmassa@drew.edu; Discussion group: poch@drew.edu)

Sh'ma Online: sponsored by *Sh'ma* Magazine
(shma@shamash.nysernet.org; contact Derek Fields
derek@bellcore.com)
UAHCampus: List for people concerned about Reform
Judaism on the college campus
(uahcampus@israel.nysernet.ORG)

More particulars:

Davka
7074 N Western Avenue
Chicago, IL 60645

The Educational Software Company (TES)
c/o Jerusalem Sales Co.
4 College Road
Monsey, NY 10452

Kabbalah Software
8 Price Drive, Dept. CJ
Edison, NJ 08817

Lev Software
P.O. Box 17832
Plantation, FL 33318

Saul Lieberman Institute of Talmudic Research
Jewish Theological Seminary of America
3080 Broadway
New York, NY 10027

Torah Educational Software
1-800-925-6853

Extra Holiday How-To
Making (International) *Charoset*
חֲרוֹסֶת

The source:

Charoset is a paste made of fruit, spices, wine, cinnamon, and nuts which forms part of the *seder* rite on the evening of Passover. It is symbolic of the mortar that the Jews made when they were slaves in Egypt. Some say that the name *charoset* is derived from the Hebrew word *cheres*, meaning "clay," because the food mixture resembles the color of clay. In Exodus 12:8 the Israelites are instructed to eat bitter herbs (*maror*). The rabbis suggested that we dip the *maror* in the *charoset* to temper the bitterness of the bitter herbs.

What you need to know:

1. Ingredients with which to make *charoset* vary from community to community. In most Western Jewish communities, *charoset* is made using apples, chopped walnuts, cinnamon, and red wine.

2. In many Sephardic communities, *charoset* is made using the biblical fruits of the Land of Israel: grapes, wheat (matzah meal), figs, olives, pomegranates, and dates.

3. Jews from North Africa often use pine nuts and hard-boiled eggs when making their *charoset*, flavoring it with piquant and pungent spices, such as ginger.

4. Jews from Yemen add other seasonings, such as chili pepper, when they make their *charoset*.

5. Israeli Jews often turn *charoset* into an actual dessert by adding bananas, dates, candied fruit peel, orange juice, and sugar.

Things to remember:

1. Be creative. Start with the basics and add the flavor of your community to the *charoset*. Make the new recipe your family's new tradition.

Key words and phrases:

Charoset. חֲרוֹסֶת Mixture eaten at Passover *seder* to symbolize mortar used to build the pyramids.

Maror. מָרוֹר Bitter herbs dipped into *charoset* over which the blessing on the herbs is said.

If you want to know more:

Philip Goodman, *The Passover Anthology* (Philadelphia, 1962).

Ronald H. Isaacs and Kerry M. Olitzky, *The Discovery Haggadah* (Hoboken, NJ, 1993).

More particulars:

Here are some international *charoset* recipes:

American *Charoset*
1 pound peeled, cored, finely chopped apples
1 cup chopped walnuts
1–2 teaspoons cinnamon (or to taste)
Sweet red wine
Add wine until mixture forms a paste, or to taste.

European *Charoset*
1 pound apples, cored and grated
1/2 cup chopped almonds or walnuts
2 tablespoons honey
1 teaspoon ground cinnamon
1/4 cup sweet red wine

Yemenite *Charoset*
15 pitted dates, chopped
15 dried figs, chopped
2 tablespoons sesame seeds (optional)
1 teaspoon ground ginger
dash of coriander
red wine to taste
1 small chili pepper or pinch of cayenne pepper (optional)

Turkish *Charoset*

1/2 cup finely chopped pitted dates
1/2 cup finely chopped figs
1/2 cup finely chopped dried apricots
1/2 cup finely chopped walnuts or almonds
1 apple, peeled, cored, and grated

Moroccan *Charoset*

1 cup chopped dates
1 cup chopped walnuts
sweet red wine to taste

Greek *Charoset*

1/2 cup black currants, finely chopped
1/2 cup raisins, finely chopped
1/2 cup almonds or pine nuts, finely chopped
1/2 cup dates, finely chopped
2 tablespoons honey (optional)
sweet red wine to taste

The source:

The commandments in the Scroll of Esther to observe Purim as a day of feasting and gladness (Esther 9:22) gave rise to the creation of many delicacies for this festival. The traditions of having a Purim *seudah* (meal) and *mishlo'ach manot* (sending gifts of food) resulted in the introduction of many new Purim delicacies. One of the most popular is *hamantaschen*, baked dough filled with poppy seeds. Because of the association of this pastry with Purim, its original name, *mohntaschen*, from the German *mohn* (poppy seed) and *taschen* (pockets), was revised to *hamantaschen*, recalling Haman, the enemy of the Jews in the Persian empire.

What you need to know:

1. Some people have suggested that the three-cornered shape of the *hamantaschen* is meant to recall the distinctive hat worn by Haman as prime minister of Persia.

2. In recent years, many new kinds of *hamantaschen* fillings have been introduced. These include prunes, cherries, and even cream cheese and chocolate chips (our favorite)!

3. There are many different recipes for baking *hamantaschen*. Here is one of our favorites:

1 pound vegetable shortening
5 cups flour
1 teaspoon salt
1 cup pineapple juice
1/2 cup sugar
Mix and refrigerate roll of sugared flour. Cut and fill. Bake at 400 degrees for 20–25 minutes.

Cream Cheese Filling
3/4 cup brown sugar

198

3 ounces cream cheese
1/2 teaspoon salt (may be omitted)
1 teaspoon vanilla
1/2 cup nuts, chocolate chips (our favorite), coconut, or peanut brittle.
Best if chilled. Mix all ingredients. Fill dough and bake.

Things to remember:

1. It is a good idea to give yourself plenty of time when preparing the *hamantaschen* for your food baskets as well as your Purim meal.

2. Be as creative as possible, and try to create your own original *hamantaschen* recipe.

3. Another favorite traditional Purim dish is *kreplach*, triangular pieces of dough filled with chopped meat. Purim shares the eating of *kreplach* with the evening of the Day of Atonement; meat is often viewed as a symbol of God's stern judgment.

4. In some places it is also customary to eat *nahit*, cooked chickpeas. This vegetarian dish recalls Esther's diet while she lived in the court of Ahasuerus. According to tradition, she ate vegetables in order not to violate the Jewish dietary laws.

Key words and phrases:

Hamantaschen. הָמָן־טַאשֶׁן/הָמָנְטַאשֶׁן Triangular Purim pastries.

Mishlo'ach manot. מִשְׁלֹחַ מָנוֹת Sending of gifts, often food baskets, to one's friends and the needy.

Oznai Haman. אָזְנֵי הָמָן Literally, "Haman's ears." Hebrew name for *hamantaschen*.

Purim seudah. סְעוּדַת פּוּרִים Purim feast, characterized by frivolity and merrymaking.

If you want to know more:

Philip Goodman, *The Purim Anthology* (Philadelphia, 1973).

Ronald H. Isaacs and Kerry M. Olitzky, *Sacred Celebrations: A Jewish Holiday Handbook* (Hoboken, NJ, 1994).

Extra Holiday How-To
Making *Etrog* Jam
רִבָּה שֶׁל אֶתְרוֹג

The source:

"On the first day, you shall take the fruit of the hadar tree, branches of the palm tree, boughs of leafy trees, and willows of the brook" (Leviticus 23:40).

What you need to know:

The *etrog* is one of the four species that are part of the ritual for Sukkot. At the end of the holiday it can be used to make jam.

Ingredients
1 *etrog*
2 lemons
1 cup preserving sugar

1. Slice the fruit into thin cross-sections. Remove the pits and white membranes as far as possible.

2. Place the fruit into a bowl of tepid water for three days. Change the water daily. (This removes some of the bitterness.) On the third day, taste the water. If it is not acidic, the fruit is ready.

3. Dry the fruit with a paper towel. (Water will retard the set of the jam.)

4. Add enough water to the sugar to cover. Then cook it over a low heat. Be careful not to burn the sugar (or yourself). Add the softened lemon slices and several teaspoons of water. When the sugar is syrupy, add the *etrog*. Continue cooking until the *etrog* gets glossy.

5. Test the jam for a set with a sugar thermometer (about 220°F. or 104°C.). As an alternative, take a few small plates; put them in the freezer for a few minutes with a spoonful of jam on each plate. (Remember to take the

jam off the stove while you are testing.) If the jam puckers and has formed a thin skin when you push it with a spoon, then it is ready. If not, cook it for a few more minutes.

6. Let the jam cool. Then place it in a jar. It should keep for up to two years.

Things to remember:

1. Try to use an *etrog* that is just underripe.

2. Use preserving sugar, not brown or white sugar.

Key words and phrases:

Etrog. אֶתְרוֹג Citron.
Pitam. פִּטָם Stemlike protrusion on the bottom of the *etrog*.

If you want to know more:

Ronald H. Isaacs and Kerry M. Olitzky, *Sacred Celebrations* (Hoboken, NJ, 1994).

Sending *Mishlo'ach Manot*

מִשְׁלֹחַ מָנוֹת

The source:

"On those days, the Jews rested from their enemies, the month was turned from sorrow to gladness, from mourning to joy. Thus, they should make them days of feasting and exhilaration, sending portions to one another and gifts to the poor" (Esther 9:22).

What you need to know:

1. Send money to the poor, and food, pastries, and something to drink to friends, as an expression of joy over Esther's victory and the survival of the Jewish people.

2. There is no need to be fancy or expensive. Send raisins, fruits, and nuts. You may also want to include something about celebrating Purim for your friends. You can include a *gragger* (noisemaker).

3. It's nice to deliver the goodies yourself or leave them on neighbors' doorsteps so that they can find them when they return home.

Things to remember:

1. Send two food items for *mishlo'ach manot* to at least one person and give *tzedakah* to the poor (*matanot la'evyonim*). Try to give your *tzedakah* on Purim itself. If this is not possible, do so later. Make it a family *mitzvah*. Decide where you want the money to go and then deliver it yourself. With all the homeless and hungry on the streets of our cities, it shouldn't be too difficult to deliver the *tzedakah* directly to people in need.

2. Make sure to include pastries relevant to the festival of Purim, like *hamantaschen*.

Key words and phrases:

Matanot la'evyonim. מַתָּנוֹת לָאֶבְיוֹנִים Gifts to the poor, mandated as part of the observance of Purim.

Mishlo'ach manot. מִשְׁלֹחַ מָנוֹת The sending of portions, often referred to as *shalach manos* by Ashkenazim and Yiddish speakers.

If you want to know more:

Ronald Isaacs and Kerry Olitzky, *Sacred Celebrations: A Jewish Holiday Handbook* (Hoboken, NJ, 1994).

More particulars:

Some congregations use *mishloach manot* baskets as fund-raisers for sisterhood, brotherhood (men's club), or youth groups.

Extra Holiday How-To
Making Cheese Blintzes
בְּלִינְצִים

The source:

Two sources have been suggested as the primary explanation for eating dairy products on Shavuot: (1) "Your lips, O my bride, drop honey; honey and milk are under your tongue" (Song of Songs 4:11). This is an allusion to the sweetness of Torah. Thus, children traditionally begin learning on Shavuot with honey dripped on the pages of text. (2) "Bring to Adonai's house the choicest first fruits. You shall not seethe a kid in its mother's milk" (Exodus 23:19). The juxtaposition of these texts suggests a relationship between Shavuot and dairy.

What you need to know:

Cheese blintzes are a traditional Shavuot food. Here is how to make them:

Batter
3 eggs (or egg substitutes for the cholesterol conscious)
2 tablespoons oil, plus additional oil for frying (not for the fat-free dieter)
1-1/4 cups milk (you can use skim)
1-1/2 tablespoons sugar
dash of salt
1. In a large bowl, mix together eggs, oil, and milk.
2. Stir in the flour, sugar, and salt.
3. In a 7-inch frying pan, heat a very small amount of oil.
4. Pour in just enough batter to cover the bottom of the pan lightly.
5. Fry for 1 minute, until the bottom of the blintze shell is light brown.
6. Remove the blintze from the pan and place it on a paper towel to drain.
7. Repeat frying process until all of the batter is used. This recipe makes about 12 blintzes.

Filling

1 pound dry cottage cheese
1/4 cup sour cream
1 egg white, beaten
dash of cinnamon
1/2 teaspoon vanilla flavoring

1. In a large bowl, mix filling ingredients together.
2. Place a tablespoon of filling in the center of each blintze (on the brown side, since the other side will become brown when the blintzes are baked.
3. Wrap the blintze around the filling like a jelly roll, then fold sides in so that the filling can't fall out.
4. Bake on a greased cookie sheet in a preheated oven at 350° F. for 30 minutes.
5. Serve hot with sour cream and jam or let cool, freeze, then reheat and serve at a later time.

Things to remember:

1. Another explanation for the association of cheese blintzes with Shavuot relates to the fact that it was on Shavuot that the Torah was given to Israel. Normally so auspicious an event would have been celebrated with a meat meal, but on the first Shavuot this was not possible, because the Israelites had not previously known the dietary laws and therefore had no supply of kosher meat readily available. Thus they had to make do with dairy.

2. Other traditional Shavuot foods include kreplach, because the three sides of this triangular-shaped food symbolize the triad of Torah-God-Israel. Cheesecake is also a popular item on this occasion. Many people also use dairy foods for their first meal after the Yom Kippur fast.

If you want to know more:

Hanna Goodman, *Jewish Cooking from Around the World* (Philadelphia, 1969).

More particulars:

Some suggest that two cheese blintzes represent the two tablets of the Ten Commandments. Two *challot* are used during Shavuot for the same reason.

Extra Holiday How-To
Making a Tu Bishevat *Seder*
סֵדֶר לְט"וּ בִּשְׁבָט

The source:

Sixteenth-century Kabbalists gathered on the eve of Tu Bishevat for singing, dancing, and the tasting of fruits and wines.

What you need to know:

1. To prepare for the Tu Bishevat *seder,* you will need the following:

    a. Red and white wine or grape juice, enough to serve each person four cups.

    b. *Seder* fruit plates. You will need three platters of fruits.

       Choose at least five with an inedible shell: tangerine, kiwi, walnut, pomegranate, pistachio, grapefruit, coconut, almond, orange.

       Choose at least five fruits with an inedible seed: peach, avocado, olive, apricot, plum, date, cherry, mango.

       Choose at least five fruits which are completely edible: grape, fig, apple, raisin, cranberry, pear, carob.

       These fruits should be cut into pieces in advance of the *seder.*

2. Serve four cups of wine during the Tu Bishevat *seder.* For the first cup, use entirely white wine or juice, which symbolizes the winter. The second cup is a mixture of white wine and a bit of red wine, symbolic of the thawing earth. The third cup has red wine with a bit of white wine, reflecting the flowers blooming in the summer. The fourth and last cup uses all red wine, suggesting the beginning of autumn.

3. Recite the blessing before drinking each cup:

בָּרוּךְ אַתָּה יהוה אֱלֹהֵינוּ מֶלֶךְ הָעוֹלָם, בּוֹרֵא פְּרִי הַגֶּפֶן:

Baruch atah Adonai elohaynu melech ha'olam borei p'ri ha'gafen.

Praised are You, Adonai our God, Sovereign of the Universe, who creates the fruit of the vine.

Now all drink the wine.

4. After each cup of wine, recite the blessing, then taste the fruit.

בָּרוּךְ אַתָּה יהוה אֱלֹהֵינוּ מֶלֶךְ הָעוֹלָם, בּוֹרֵא פְּרִי הָעֵץ:

Baruch atah Adonai elohaynu melech ha'olam borei p'ri ha'etz.

Praised are You, Adonai our God, Sovereign of the Universe, who creates the fruit of trees.

Now share the fruit.

5. Sometime during the *seder* you may want to invite someone to ask Four Questions about the *seder*. All of these questions should focus on the theme of trees and fruit, growth and ecology. For example, someone might ask: On all of the other days of the year we rarely mention the importance of trees and fruit. Why on this day do we think of fruit and trees?

6. Each participant needs a Tu Bishevat Haggadah. There are a variety of different *seder* booklets designed for Tu Bishevat that will assist you in conducting your own *seder*. Feel free to make your own.

Things to remember:

1. There is a tradition which suggests that trees are judged by God on Tu Bishevat just as all people are judged on Rosh Hashanah. That is why Tu Bishevat is also called the New Year for Trees.

2. In Israel, Tu Bishevat is an official holiday, involving elaborate parades, songs, and general merriment.

3. The organization that works to reforest Israel is the Jewish National Fund (JNF).

4. In addition to having a Tu Bishevat *seder,* you may want to consider an activity such as maple sugar sapping. (Check with your community park service to see whether this is permitted.)

5. There is a custom of giving multiples of 91 cents to various charities on Tu Bishevat. In gematria, 91 is the numerical equivalent for the Hebrew word for "tree" (*ilan*).

Key words and phrases:

Keren Kayemet L'Yisrael. קֶרֶן קַיֶמֶת לְיִשְׂרָאֵל Hebrew name of the Jewish National Fund.

Rosh Hashanah La'ilanot. רֹאש הַשָׁנָה לָאִילָנוֹת New Year for Trees; another name for Tu Bishevat.

If you want to know more:

Harlene Winnick Appelman et al., *A Seder for Tu Bishevat* (Baltimore, 1984).

Adam Fisher, *Seder Tu Bishevat: The Festival of Trees* (New York, 1989).

Voice of the Trees. This is the newspaper of Shomrei Adamah, a Jewish organization devoted to ecology and the environment. Write them at Church Road and Greenwood Avenue, Wyncote, PA 19095, for information.

More particulars:

Here are several Tu Bishevat table songs to sing at your Tu Bishevat *seder.*

> 1. *Hashkediya porachat*
> *V'shemesh paz zorachat*
> *Tziporim merosh kol gag*
> *M'vasrot et bo hechag*
> *Tu Bishevat higiyah Chag ha'ilanot* (2)
>
> The almond tree is growing
> A golden sun is glowing
> Birds sing out in joyous glee
> From every roof and every tree.
> Tu Bishevat is here
> The Jewish Arbor Day
> Hail the trees' New Year
> Happy holiday.

2. *Tzaddik katamar yifrach yifrach*
K'erez ba'levanon yisgeh
Shetulim bevayt Hashem.

Righteous people will grow mightly like the palm and flourish like the cedars of Lebanon.

3. *Atzay zaytim omdim la la la . . .*

The olive trees are standing.

4. *Eytz chayyim hee la'machazikim bah ve'tomcheha me'ushar*
Deracheha darchay no'am ve'chol netivoteha shalom.
Hasheevaynu Adonai eylecha ve'nashuvah chadesh ya-maynu ke'kedem.

It is a tree of life to those who hold fast to it, and those who uphold it are happy. Its ways are ways of pleasantness and all its paths turn to peace. Return us to You, O God, and we shall return. Renew our days as of old.

5. *Eytz chayyim hee la'machazikim bah ve'tomcheha me'ushar. Deracheha darchay no'am ve'chol netivoteha shalom.*

It is a tree of life to those who hold fast to it, and those who uphold it are happy. Its ways are ways of pleasantness and all its paths turn to peace. Shalom

209

Extra Holiday How-to
Dipping Apples in Honey
(and Not Getting Stuck)
תַפּוּחִים

The source:

On Rosh Hashanah, people customarily eat apples dipped in honey. This custom symbolically expresses the hope that there will be many sweet times in the coming year. We will all learn ways of being sweeter in everything we say and do (*Turei Zahav*, chap. 583).

What you need to know:

1. It is customary to eat apples and honey on the eve of Rosh Hashanah before the festive meal.

2. Take apples, cut them into pieces, and give a piece to each member of the family. Dip the apples into the honey, then say the following blessings before eating the apples and honey.

יְהִי רָצוֹן מִלְּפָנֶיךָ יְיָ אֱלֹהֵינוּ וֵאלֹהֵי אֲבוֹתֵינוּ שֶׁתְּחַדֵּשׁ עָלֵינוּ שָׁנָה טוֹבָה וּמְתוּקָה.

Yehi ratzon milfanecha Adonai elohaynu vaylohay avotenu she-te-cha-desh alaynu shanah tova u'metukah.

May it be Your will, Adonai our God, that You renew for us a good and sweet year.

בָּרוּךְ אַתָּה יהוה אֱלֹהֵינוּ מֶלֶךְ הָעוֹלָם, בּוֹרֵא פְּרִי הָעֵץ:

Baruch atah Adonai elohaynu melech ha'olam boray p'ri ha'etz.

Praised are You, Adonai, our God, Sovereign of the Universe, who creates the fruit of the tree.

Things to remember:

1. Many families go apple picking before the festival of Rosh Hashanah. Some wait for the week of Sukkot. It is a nice idea to pick extra apples and give them to a local food bank.

2. There are many biblical references to honey, one of the sweetest products of nature. The Land of Israel is called the land of milk and honey in the Bible (Exodus 3:8). Bees are still abundant even in the remote parts of Israel's desert, where they deposit their honey in the crevices of rocks or in hollow trees. Honey was not to be used in sacrifices (Leviticus 2:11), but the first fruits of honey, as of other kinds of produce, were to be presented to God, for the use by God's priests. Here are some of the other biblical references to honey:

> a. "On that day I lifted My hand to them, to bring them out of Egypt into a land flowing with milk and honey" (Ezekiel 20:6).
> b. "And the House of Israel called its name manna, and it was like coriander seed, white. Its taste was like wafers made with honey" (Exodus 16:31).
> c. "Then Jonathan said, 'How my eyes are brightened, because I have tasted a little of this honey'" (I Samuel 14:29).
> d. "More to be desired are the ordinances of God than much fine gold, sweeter also than honey and the honeycomb" (Psalm 19:10).
> e. "My child, eat honey, for it is good, and the honeycomb is sweet to your taste" (Proverbs 24:13).

Key words and phrases:

D'vash. דְּבַשׁ Honey.
Shanah tovah. שָׁנָה טוֹבָה Happy New Year.

If you want to know more:

Philip Goodman, *The Rosh Hashanah Anthology* (Philadelphia, 1973).
Arthur I. Waskow, *Seasons of Our Joy* (New York, 1982).

Life-Cycle Checklists

BRIT MILAH AND NAMING PLANS (including *Simchat Bat*)

This list will help you to keep track of the organization for your *Brit Milah* and naming plans.

___Date and time of birth _____
___Date and time of *Brit Milah* _____
___Date and time of naming ceremony _____
___Name of *mohel/mohelet* or Jewish physician _____
___Officiating clergy _____
___Hebrew/Jewish name for our child _____
___We have notified all of our guests.
___We have selected for our twinning ceremony.
___The *kvater* is _____
___The *kvaterin* is _____
___The *sandek* is _____
___We have arranged for a *shalom zachor/nekevah* which will take place at _____.
___We have arranged for the *seudat mitzvah.*
___Our participants at the *seudat mitzvah* will be _____to lead *Hamotzi* over the bread and _____to lead the *Birkat Hamazon* (grace after the meal).

PIDYON HABEN/HABAT

This list will help you to keep track of your plans for organizing a *Pidyon Haben/Habat.*

___Date and time of *Pidyon Haben/Habat* _____
___Name of officiating clergy _____
___Name of *kohen* _____
___We have contacted all of our guests.
___We have obtained five silver shekels (silver dollars).
___We have arranged for the *seudat mitzvah.*
___*Kiddush* (blessing over the wine) will be recited by ___
___*Hamotzi* (blessings over the bread) will be said by ___
___*Birkat Hamazon* (grace after the meal) will be led by _

BAR/BAT MITZVAH

This list will help you to keep track of the organization for your Bar/Bat Mitzvah.

___Hebrew/English date of Bar/Bat Mitzvah _____
___Names(s) of Torah portion and Haftarah _____

___I have sent out invitations

___Name of person with whom twinning will take place _

___Name of florist _____

___Name of photographer _____

___Name of caterer _____

___We have selected our participants in the service and reminded those that will chant blessings to review them. They are:

Ark Openers and Closers

(English Names) _____

(Hebrew Names) _____

Aliyot:

___ 1. English and Hebrew name: _____

___ 2. English and Hebrew name: _____

___ 3. English and Hebrew name: _____

___ 4. English and Hebrew name: _____

___ 5. English and Hebrew name: _____

___ 6. English and Hebrew name: _____

___ 7. English and Hebrew name: _____

___ 8. (*Maftir*) Bar/Bat Mitzvah: English and Hebrew name: _____

___*Hagbahah* (lift Torah): English and Hebrew name: ___

___*Gelilah* (dress Torah): English and Hebrew name: ___

Other parts in service: Name _____ Part _____

___Name of *Kiddush* chanter _____

___Name of person leading *Hamotzi* _____

___Name of person leading *Birkat Hamazon* (grace after the meal) _____

___List of new *mitzvot* that Bar/Bat Mitzvah will consider doing the first year:

1. _____

2. _____

3. _____

4. _____

5. _____

___*Tzedakah* organizations for contributions: _____

_____

A JEWISH WEDDING

This list will help you to keep track of your wedding plans:

___Wedding date _____

___Officiants _____

___Place of wedding _____
___Place of reception _____
___Our meeting with the rabbi/cantor will take place on
___We have selected our wedding ring(s).
___We have ordered our wedding invitations.
___We have selected our *chuppah.*
___We have selected our *ketubah.*
___Our two witnesses will be _____
___Our attendants will be: Best man_____
　　　　Maid/Matron of honor _____
___Our other attendants in our wedding procession are:
___We have chosen these musical selections: _____
_____
___We have taken our blood tests and applied for the civil license.
___We have arranged for an *aufruf.*
___We have arranged for an organization that will use food left over from the reception _____.
___In honor of our wedding, we will contribute *tzedakah* to these organizations:
_____

CLERGY CARD FOR FUNERAL
___English/Hebrew name of deceased _____
___English/Hebrew date of death _____
___Officiating clergyperson _____
___Name and location of cemetery _____
___Location of plot in cemetery _____
___Names of pallbearers
_____
_____
_____
_____
_____
_____
___Contact person for the cemetery _____
___Funeral Home _____
___Contact person at the funeral home _____
___Contact person for the Chevra Kaddisha _____